LECTURES AND PLAY

A Practical and Fun Guide to Create Extraordinary Higher Education Classroom Experiences

LECTURES AND PLAY

A PRACTICAL AND FUN GUIDE TO CREATE EXTRAORDINARY HIGHER EDUCATION CLASSROOM EXPERIENCES

Dr. SILVIANA FALCON

NEW DEGREE PRESS

LECTURES AND PLAY
A Practical and Fun Guide to Create Extraordinary Higher Education Classroom Experiences

ISBN 978-1-63730-441-9 *Paperback*
978-1-63730-539-3 *Kindle Ebook*
978-1-63730-540-9 *Ebook*

For our Students

TABLE OF CONTENTS

AUTHOR'S NOTE

Preface

COVID-19 forced us to think again about every aspect of education from kindergarten to higher education. This was the force that broke the system we all knew was killing our student's love for learning and our love for teaching. Hooray—at last, it is broken. However, let us not put the pieces back together. Let us agree to do the hard work of examining what each one of us can do to make a difference. Then, we must hold ourselves and each other accountable to bring back education in a way that allows us to engage students in the learning process, thus motivating them to learn, focus, and engage in higher-level critical thinking.

Each one of us has the power, knowledge, skill, and ability to change our educational system from within. If we have the courage and the passion to break with convention, we can produce students who will not only become more efficient critical thinkers, but who will also incorporate our disruptive model as the new conventional model to higher education. I do get it—with our ever-increasing workload, it is easier and comforting to go back to replicate the pedagogy that we and others before us used. Let us have the courage and the passion to break with convention.

The goal of this book is to serve as a guide to inspire and challenge you to make a conscious movement toward a more active, visual presentation of material as a way to complement your rich lectures.

In the pages that follow, I make a case for incorporating games to your lectures and offer a collection of simple, tested-and-tried engaged learning activities. These unique activities present a range of possible designs and their amazing value. This collection of outstanding games and activities can be used to teach more than a single subject or principle. May this information inspire you to explore, create, and try new things.

INTRODUCTION

"The mind is not a vessel that needs filling, but wood that needs igniting."

PLUTARCK

As a fairly new academic, I received a note from a student at the end of my course that read, "I was so quiet in high school—you encouraged me to use my voice in class. I haven't had a teacher notice me, and you even believed in me."

After reading her note and subsequently talking with the student about her experience in my class, it became painfully evident that the educational model had not changed much since my college years. She shared that she entered college thinking that being a good student meant to sit quietly, take notes, and memorize efficiently to perform well at an end-of-the-year multiple choice exam. At least, that was the framework she perfected over her K-12 educational journey. She mentioned that my classroom environment allowed her not only to think and reflect, but to envision herself as a leader.

Since our conversation, she has been an active creator of her destiny. She successfully participated in two internships with nationally and internationally renowned finance corporations and became an active, executive member of several student organizations.

After this experience, I began pondering about our education system and its reliance on a pedagogy that aims at having students absorb as much information as possible, and rewards passive learning. In conversations with other professors, I learned that many of them actually do not believe in this type of pedagogy. Without a doubt, most professors want their students to be passionate, lifelong learners. We desire to nurture our students so they are prepared to lead their families, communities, and our world. Frankly, these are difficult outcomes for anyone to achieve. I believe this is where the sacredness, importance, and difficulty of our profession becomes evident.

If we look beyond the classroom, we find evidence of how passive learning has a negative impact on the US workforce. According to Brandon Busteed, 96 percent of higher education officials believe their institutions are very or somewhat effective at preparing students for the workforce; however, only 11 percent of business leaders strongly agree (Busteed, 2014). This is extremely important as major industries are unable to grow and compete due to the lack of properly skilled talent. Higher education rewards individual achievement, memorization, and the ability to follow. In contrast, innovative work environments place value on teamwork, independent thinking, and effective communication. There is a total disconnect with the predictable outcomes we are experiencing.

In 2017, the U.S. Chamber of Commerce Foundation (USCCF) produced a report titled "Learning to Work, Working to Learn" highlighting best practices in the alignment of higher education with the workforce. Their recommendation was to use project-based or simulated experiences to leverage collaboration, communication, and critical thinking skills.

The power of simulated experiences (or active inquiry) in education as a transformative tool has been well-established. In fact, during the past few decades, the traditional lecture has come under increasing criticism as mounting evidence confirms that most students learn better by engaging with content and reflecting upon it, a method commonly referred to as "active learning" (Hake, 1998; National Research Council 2000, Prince, 2004; Knight and Wood, 2005; Handelsman et al., 2007; Freeman et al., 2014; Deslauriers et al., 2019, Petersen et al 2020, Forbes, 2021). Interestingly, Deslauriers et al. took their research a step further by comparing student learning of a specific set of topics at an introductory undergraduate physics course, using two different instructional approaches (Deslauriers et al., 2019). One group of students (N=267), was taught using the traditional lecture given by an experienced and highly rated instructor. The second group of students (N=271), was taught by a trained but highly inexperienced professor using research-based instruction. The researchers found that students had a higher level of engagement, increased attendance, and more than twice the level of learning with the highly inexperienced professor who used research-based instruction.

With all of this mounting evidence, why does the educational system sustain a passive learning model? Well, passive learning holds the student responsible for content acquisition. The student is accountable for paying attention, listening, and writing notes and enhancing convergent thinking, where a given question typically has only one right answer. Passive learning allows the professor more control over the content delivery, especially when the number of students in an introductory course can easily reach over a hundred. One of the main problems with passive learning is the assessment of student comprehension only takes place during exams, minimizing the student's involvement in the learning experience.

Contrary to passive learning, active learning, via games and challenges, helps activate divergent thinking and allows students to think in terms of the big picture. Active learning increases the student's ability to think critically by stimulating discussions. Other skills gained by active learning are teamwork, analysis, public speaking, and collaboration; the very skills innovative employers are looking for. Additionally, active learning methods allow the professor to assess their students' understanding because there is constant feedback about the material between the student and the professor.

I believe both approaches are useful. Students must gain new knowledge and skills. Passive learning caters to knowledge acquisition more than exploration. Active learning, on the other hand, is best used when exploration and finding connections are the goal. Active learning emphasizes the ability of both professors and students to rediscover the magic of education, where information is exciting, and the anticipation of new discoveries is liberating.

I believe, in order to create dynamic and inviting learning experiences, both passive and active teaching methods must be incorporated to ensure better student engagement. Initial knowledge transfer requires passive learning. However, higher education should also be all about gaining deeper insights about oneself and about the world, and that is exactly where active learning becomes an integral component to learning.

The purpose of higher education is to teach students complex subjects, to help them learn to think, analyze, explore new ideas, to ask questions, and to develop a desire for learning and exploration. By design, the use of an exclusive passive learning pedagogy falls short in achieving this purpose. It comes as no surprise that our graduates are not consistently meeting the critical thinking expectations employers want.

I am compelled to write about the blending of active and passive learning in higher education because the outcome of my work has been astounding. For example, I have students showing up at 7:45 a.m. for an 8:00 a.m. course with consistent 100 percent attendance.

The classroom experience from a student's perspective is summarized in this course evaluation comment, "Loved this class and I really felt like I learned practical skills. Sometimes in classes, there is not enough emphasis on the practical application or why what we are learning matters. I really liked how this class did not revolve around just reading a textbook and discussing. We played games and had fluid discussions and watched videos and heard personal examples, and that was much more effective to my learning in the class than just working from a textbook would have been."

Since incorporating more educational games and stories into my lectures, I have found my teaching to be more effective. I also truly had fun doing it. The activities allow me to sit with smaller groups of students and respond to questions they initiate. It allows me the unique opportunity to listen to their way of thinking.

Most of us use student course evaluations as one of the metrics to assess our teaching effectiveness. Since the introduction of educational games to my lectures, my course evaluations consistently place my overall teaching performance at 6.9 out of 7.0. These high scores provide me the encouragement and motivation to keep innovating new ways to present material. The fears that kept me from trying something different never came to be—quite the contrary. My efforts were recently recognized when I was awarded two of the highest honors bestowed by my academic institution for excellence in teaching.

While the scores and the recognition are something I am deeply grateful for, just like many of my colleagues, I am always assessing if my teaching has had any transformative power in the lives of my students beyond the classroom. To date, my students invariably report a sense of purpose, a direction for their learning, and a desire to learn more. They describe an understanding of the various concepts and the reasons why they are important in their lives and the lives of others.

For example, one student wrote, "Co-workers have commented that recently I have started saying things that have begun to inspire them to improve too. Dr. Falcon inspired me to inspire others and I want her to know that she has improved the lives of people beyond her classroom...I have decided to explore earning a master's degree in business and/or work towards becoming a departmental manager in my office. I started with a goal to pass a class, I ended with a goal to improve my world."

This is one of many student comments that have inspired me to continue to innovate and create educational games to complement my lectures. My goal with this book is to inspire professors not only to view educational games as serious intellectual and creative work, but to take a leap of faith and become courageous because courage is effectively contagious.

Regardless of the path you took to become a higher education professor, the fact is that empowering and inspiring with great teaching is truly an incredible feeling. We do not need to be lone genius thinkers developing a new theory about pedagogy. While that might make for good storytelling, the truth is that breakthroughs often come from people who get to a point in their day-to-day frustrations where they realize, "There has to be a better way." So they set out to create one.

If you want to engage your students more, but you are not sure where to start, this book is for you. In the pages that follow, you will find not only why engaging students works, but I have also put together a collection of simple, tried-and-tested training activities that you can use today in your classroom. These unique activities present a range of possible designs and provide contextual understanding of various concepts like the importance of planning, mentoring, teamwork, collaboration, and critical thinking. You can use this collection of outstanding games, tips, and tricks to teach more than a single subject or principle. May this information inspire you to explore, create, and try new things.

PART ONE:

WHY, WHAT, AND HOW

CHAPTER 1

WHY GAME-BASED LEARNING MATTERS

"Never let schooling get in the way of your education."

BENJAMIN FRANKLIN.

I joined the world of academia intending not to stay longer than a year. It was simply a door that opened up at a season of brokenness and distress. I had been a successful healthcare executive for more than twenty years. In 2009, I was promoted to work directly for the top two executives of the company as an internal consultant, turning troubled clinical departments into efficient and quality-driven business lines. In 2010, the top executive retired and, as expected, the new executive team had a strong vision of expansion. Over the next twelve months, I witnessed the company's rebirth. However, this time, it was being engineered with an entirely different set of objectives. The more I worked in that environment, the more I questioned who was teaching these new business leaders to be so apathetic; it seemed to me that they were focused solely on the return on investment (ROI) as opposed to the patients' or staff members' well-being, not to mention, the quality and effectiveness of the healthcare system.

For the first time in my life and despite all of my professional success, I found myself just existing. No plan. No idea how to proceed. By mid-summer of 2012, I prepared my curriculum vitae and stopped by my alma mater's adult and graduate programs office. To this day, I am not sure why I took such action. The very next day, I received a call offering me an adjunct position teaching one management class during the day. As painful as it was, I knew it was time to make a professional move. A month later, I found myself in a profession I was unsure of with a 99.9 percent salary decrease but a renewed sense of wholeness.

My one and only class met on Mondays, Wednesdays, and Fridays at 8:00 a.m. I remember arriving to the parking lot forty-five minutes before the start of class so I could have a moment to cry, silently questioning God's will for me. After all, how could something like this be happening to me? I had worked so hard to be successful in a profession I loved. I had been a faithful servant of others. I had refused to continue in a job that no longer aligned with my personal and professional values. I was a good, faithful wife and mother. Then, after a few minutes of self-pity, I cleaned up my face, put fresh makeup on, and went into the classroom asking God to help me overcome this season of adversity and failure.

Over the days and months that followed, I noticed that despite twenty years of accelerated change and increased performance expectations in the industry, not much had changed in academia. The classroom remained, for the most part, teacher-centered, and a majority of the students had learned to be passive learners. I began to pay attention to the conversations of highly regarded professors who argued there is much knowledge to transmit during a semester and thus, the only way to disseminate the material effectively is through lectures. The main complaint from these professors seemed to be that students just "do not study hard enough," or simply, "they are coming to college unprepared."

Perhaps that is the case, but why? Then, I began to understand the gap I noticed over the years with new hires. They were good at taking notes and following directions, but were ill-prepared to analyze and communicate effectively. They moved from being passive learners to passive employees.

Unfortunately, my observations were not unique. In the 2011 book *Academically Adrift: Limited Learning on College Campuses* by Richard Arum and Josipa Roksa, the authors found little to no improvement during college in critical thinking and complex reasoning as measured by the Collegiate Learning Assessment (CLA), which is a standardized test administered to students in their first semester and then again at the end of their second year. According to their analysis of more than 2,300 undergraduate students at twenty-four institutions, 45 percent of these students demonstrated no significant improvement in a range of skills—including critical thinking, complex reasoning, and writing—during their first two years of college. Arum and Roksa argue these results were to be expected as institutional culture tends to place more emphasis on socializing than learning.

In 2013, the Wabash National Study (WNS) of Liberal Arts Education reported in an article by Ernest T. Pascarella and Charles Blaich, that pedagogy matters. They wrote, "student's exposure to clear and organized instruction enhanced not only their general cognitive skills such as critical thinking, but also their orientation toward inquiry and continuing intellectual development." It also increased student satisfaction, which led to higher student retention. They also reported, "deep learning experiences count." Learning activities that require students to apply theories and concepts to practical problems, to synthesize ideas and experiences, and to reflect on the personal meaning of an issue or concept (higher-order learning, integrative learning, and reflective learning) all lead to that elusive intellectual growth a college education should provide.

Fast forward to 2019, a survey report from the National Association of Colleges and Employers (NACE) found that "beyond a relevant major for the position and a strong GPA, problem solving skills, and the ability to work as part of a team are the attributes employers most want to see on resumes. Ninety-one percent of employer respondents are seeking signs of a candidate's problem solving skills, and 86 percent want proof of a candidate's ability to work as part of a team." Among other college graduate attributes were a strong work ethic, analytical/quantitative skills, written communication skills, leadership, and verbal communication skills. The requests from employers have remained consistent over a number of years. They want informed, educated, engaged, and thoughtful citizens. Nevertheless, should we not all be asking for the same outcome? In a technologically driven world where Siri can give us every fact known to man in a matter of a second, should we not all be focused on shifting our pedagogy to help students evaluate information, make inferences, incorporate objections and opposing views into their thinking, make decisions, and solve problems with less direction from us?

During this time of research and inquiry, my two oldest sons were also attending college at two different universities. During their winter break, we gathered along with a few of their friends after dinner and talked about their classes and their experiences thus far. They all seemed to have acclimated well to their newfound freedom while maneuvering through higher academic expectations. The conversation then shifted to their academic experience in the classroom. I recall one of them explaining how it really did not matter much if he attended class because he had access to the professor's notes or recorded lectures. Ultimately, he said, "I am having to teach the content to myself in order to pass the end of the year exam anyway." As I looked around the table, they all nodded in agreement, at what seemed like a collective experience. For them, college was about the mechanical learning of material and nothing else. This was a truly devastating moment for me that ignited a desire to change something, anything to make things better for our society, our economy, our democracy, and our world.

So, I followed up on that desire and one morning before class I started writing down everything I could imagine to be afraid of if I stepped away from this passive teaching: other professors would think I am too easy because I am having too much fun in the classroom; I will not be respected as a serious scholar; my students may not know how to engage in an active learning environment; I could fail, get fired, be a bad professor; I could be fooling myself; other professors would laugh behind my back. The possibilities were terrifying. Half a page of awful possibilities was enough to make me quit. Consciously or not, I knew my fear could not get in the way of helping my students find their voices and ultimately become active contributors to our society. It was time for me to leave my comfort zone. After all, if I became a more engaging professor, I would, in essence, be asking my students to do the very same. I also knew every step forward in my life, big or small, always began with leaving my comfort zone. Then, right before taking a step, I started thinking about the long-established culture of higher education where lectures are as sacred as the institutions themselves. Ambivalence and deep-rooted self-doubt settled in. Perhaps, my effort might make me feel better, but in the vast horizon, it wouldn't do much. Right?

One day, I typed the word fear in my search engine. I came across the book by Frances Moore Lappé and Jeffrey Perkins titled, *You Have the Power: Choosing Courage in a Culture of Fear*. I ordered it and devoured it in three days. I learned, my thinking was antiquated and needed revision. I learned action, even in my fear, allows others the freedom and courage to do the same. They tell of a powerful story of the women in the rain.

> *Thirty years ago, Women Strike for Peace helped achieve a remarkable victory: an end to above-ground nuclear testing that rained radioactive fallout worldwide, even showing up at dangerous levels in mothers' milk. Journalist Rebecca Solnit recalls hearing of a middle-aged member of the group talking about feeling utterly "foolish and futile" as she stood in the rain one morning, sign in hand, protesting at the Kennedy White House.*
>
> *Futile? Many years later, she would hear Dr. Benjamin Spock – then one of the country's highest-profile opponents of nuclear testing – say the turning-to-action point for him was seeing a small group of women standing in the*

> *rain, protesting at the White House. According to Solnit, Spock concluded, "If they were so passionately committed, he should give the issue more consideration himself."*

The story was the kick in the gut I needed to ignite my courage. I knew that courage often meant little more than taking an action, even if we are not sure it is going to work. I needed to let urgency conquer my fear. I began experimenting early and often. I intentionally developed my classroom environment to critically engage students with the aim of reducing the gap between objectives and expected outcomes. By incorporating games, stories, and activities in my lectures, I witnessed students slowly letting go of the comfort of passive learning and embracing the idea of being active participants in their learning experience.

Luckily, the college I work for encourages and expects the use of creativity to drive authentic learning. I took advantage of the invitation to innovate. While I loved lecturing with integrated videos and visual aids, I noticed students were continuing to listen and write with very little two-way communication. So, I began to research, learn, and work on developing new ways to increase collaboration, communication, and critical thinking. All the roads seemed to lead to educational games and their pedagogical value in the classroom.

In fact, research has consistently proven the pedagogical value of games in the classroom. For example, Dan Finkel found that using game simulations in the classroom allows the professor to share classroom leadership, with students evoking what he called "inquiry-based learning." Increasing students' level of engagement and motivation is vital to deep learning and enhanced learning outcomes (Finkel, 2000; Konopka et al.,

2015). Students are motivated to investigate and attempt to solve a problem through engaged participation. Lisa Forbes conducted a phenomenological study examining the students' experience of play as it relates to their learning. The themes that emerged from Dr. Forbes' research were, "1) play is underutilized and devalued in higher education; 2) play cultivated relational safety and a warm classroom environment; 3) play removes barriers to learning; 4) play awakened student's positive affect and motivation; and 5) play ignited an open and engaged learning stance to learning" (Forbes, 2021). Dr. Forbes' findings further support previous research indicating play improves social bonding and leads to positive emotions and enhanced, more memorable learning experiences (Brown, 2009).

Additional research concluded, "...during a simulation, participants unconsciously process all types of information: facts, emotions, strategies, outcomes, relationships, feelings, and much more...Learning happened because the students are active and not passive in the process" (Petranek, Corey, and Black, 1992).

Researchers looking at motivation agree that active learning plays a key role in motivating students. In fact, Orbach concluded, "active participation in simulation games is not a cause of motivation, but rather the result of it. Without motivation in the first place, there would be no active participation in the second" (Orbach, 1979).

Active participation in educational games and simulations provides an unparalleled opportunity to apply different approaches to solve the same problem. Students are not just able to see their own problem solving, but also interact with others with their own unique problem solving pathways. For this very reason, educational games provide not only the opportunity for individualized instruction, but also for immediate, individualized feedback. "Students need feedback about the degree to which they know when, where, and how to use the knowledge they are learning" (Bransford et al., 2000).

Academic games are a form of experiential learning. In the book, *Teaching for Learning*, its authors explain, academic games provide the context students need to learn new concepts. (Major et. al., 2015). While playing well-designed games, students participate and engage in the learning process. Games allow them to build strong connections to the curriculum so they can effectively retrieve the material at a later time.

In my experience, the most important feature of academic games is the impact such an approach has on the engagement among students. Games can produce an emotional connection to the material, increasing the level of engagement and commitment to the class. When students are more highly engaged, they become more motivated to learn and retain content knowledge. Introducing a competitive element can increase engagement and motivation as well, improving outcomes. It is worth noting however, the ability to add a competitive element is highly contextual and depends on the type of game being played.

All this talk about the advantages and features of game-based learning wouldn't mean much if game-based learning didn't have strong outcomes. Fortunately, research has shown game-based learning can have multiple positive outcomes for students. According to a report released by three researchers, Vandercruysse, Vandeaetere, and Calrebout, game-based learning is correlated with improved attitudes toward subjects students often dislike, such as math. Students also showed a general enjoyment of games, including educational games.

It is of critical importance to note, for the educational games to be effective, they should relate to a course-learning objective and provide a level of engagement and fun. In my experience, students are willing to invest their time and energy in play and games because they are intrinsically motivated to do so and can learn without even realizing it. Indeed, as Stuart Brown (2019) explained:

"During play, the brain is making sense of itself through simulation and testing. Play activity is actually helping sculpt the brain. In play, most of the time, we are able to try out things without threatening our physical or emotional well-being. We are safe precisely because we are playing."

For humans, creating such simulations of life may be play's most valuable benefit. In play, we can experience situations we have never encountered before and learn from them. We can create possibilities that have never existed, but may in the future. We make new cognitive connections find their way into our everyday lives. We can learn lessons and skills without being directly at risk.

In other words, play matters a lot to our learning and development. Stuart Brown eloquently brings it to life during his 2005 TED Talk titled, "Play Is More Than Just Fun." In it, he explains, if you take rats and allow a group to continue to squeak and wrestle each other during their juvenile years and take another group—the experimental group—and suppress their ability to play, and you present both groups of rats with a cat odor-saturated collar, they both react the same: they flee and hide as they are hardwired to do so (Brown, 2005). According to Brown, what happens next objectifies what play does, at least in the animal world. The non-playing rats never come out. They die. The players, on the other hand, slowly explore the environment and begin again to test things out. Exploration or a sense of curiosity is possible because it, "allow(s) us to take in novelty and newness, use it to adapt and become more flexible, and also have a good time in the process."

Could we objectify what play (or absence of play) does for humans? Is play important to our ability to be critical thinkers and problem solvers? Dr. Stuart Brown's, TED Talk, also shares a powerful story about the California's Institute of Technology Jet Propulsion Laboratory's (JPL) experience. As the leading center for robotic exploration of the solar system, it began to see a troubling pattern emerge among its new researchers and scientists not seen among the retiring group that had been hired in the 1960s. Undoubtedly, the new engineers coming from MIT, Stanford, and CalTech excelled with theoretical and mathematical problems, but had difficulty taking a complex project from theory to practice. "Unlike their elders, the young engineers couldn't spot the key flaws in one of the complex systems they were working on, or toss the problem around, break it down, pick it apart, tease out its critical elements, and rearrange them in innovative ways that led to a solution."

The main difference between the retiring engineers and their young counterparts was, "in their youth, their older, problem solving, research-based employees had taken apart clocks to see how they worked, or made soapbox derby racers, or built hi-fi stereos, or had fixed appliances. The young engineering school graduates, who had also done these things, who had played with their hands, were adept at the kinds of problem-solving that management sought. Those who had not generally were not. From that point on, JPL-NASA made questions about applicants' youthful projects and hand-play a standard part of job interviews." Today, JPL offers a year-round internship program offering undergraduate and graduate students the opportunity to keep building things with their hands.

In a recent book from Joshua Eyler titled, *How Humans Learn,* he shares his findings from exploring what is known from the fields of psychology, evolutionary biology, and neuroscience in regards to how humans learn (Eyler, 2018). His approach is unique as it places science in the middle of classroom practices. His extensive research of the literature led him to notice there are some patterns on how humans learn, and he outlined the following factors as instrumental to our learning: curiosity, sociality, emotion, authenticity, and failure. Eyler points out, we can grow curiosity by allowing discussion as well as activities where students create their own questions. He further explains, not only are we curious, but we have a strong desire to belong and develop deep connections with other people. Thus, "the classroom is the most immediate place where a student should feel like she or he belongs to a community of learners" (Eyler, 2018).

Curiosity and sociality can be further enhanced by exerting positive emotions from students by incorporating humor and providing real life context (authenticity) to our teaching.

Lastly, as higher education professors, adding an element for students to learn from failure is pivotal to their learning. Our classrooms provide an element of safety, as the stakes are low while we provide guidance and mentoring for them to gain valuable knowledge from their errors and misconceptions. We have the opportunity to teach what we know best as scholars and academics, the power of the iterative process.

I believe weaving a game or story into our rich lectures allows us the opportunity to add the dimensions of curiosity, sociality, emotion, authenticity, and failure, Eyler describes over and over again through the course of the semester. For example, one of the games I adapted to the classroom setting early on, and have continued to use quite successfully, is the Effectiveness and Efficiency Game (further described in the game section of this book). I was introduced to the game as a way to learn and subsequently apply lean manufacturing principles in healthcare. The game is used in the industry to highlight the need for variation reduction, productivity, reduced waste. I use the game to help students understand the power of teamwork, coaching and mentoring, informal power, motivation, time studies, and, of course, effectiveness and efficiency. The game also allows me to establish an opportunity to pique students' interest in the subject, create a community and authenticity, establish a positive environment where students are having fun and feel happy and energized, all while experiencing failure and improvement through the application of the iterative process.

The game uses four sheets of paper with numbers 1 to 100 scattered on the page in various orientations, fonts, and font sizes. I share with students I was just hired as their new manager and the previous three managers had been fired due to the inability to meet production goals. Students are given sixty seconds to circle as many numbers they can find and must do so in a consecutive order. After the first round, most students typically find up to ten numbers. I have them report out their initial score.

I take time to praise the student who had the highest score. Then, I ask if he/she would be willing to mentor other great team members who may be struggling a bit. Then, I invite the lowest-scoring students to move closer to the highest-scoring team member. I always receive willingness from the under-performing team member to collaborate. By the time we play the fourth round, students are energized and, via lean principles, their ability to achieve success is clearly established.

The students gain significant self-confidence as the game is played. Among the takeaways for the students is the overwhelming feeling of success through cooperation and teamwork. They also speak about the importance of having a person help them be successful and how getting closer and closer to meeting the goal motivated them to try harder.

The Effectiveness and Efficiency Game is one of many games I play ahead of the lecture. In doing so, I am able to recall some of the comments and situations the students experienced during the game as a way to provide another opportunity for them to connect the new material with their experience. I have also found the practice of front-ending the games increases the overall energy in the classroom. Students tend to continue in that mode, becoming much more active during the lecture. The success of the Effectiveness and Efficiency game inspired me to incorporate games into each of my lectures.

The following are comments from students at the end of my first academic year:

"This business class was just a GenEd, so I didn't care too much for the subject; however, Dr. Falcon increased my interest and made me understand the topics very well. Dr. Falcon is one of the good ones. She is an A+++ professor at Florida Southern College."

"Dr. Falcon is fantastic. I can honestly say she was my favorite teacher this semester and probably one of the best I've ever had at any school. I hope I will be able to take another class with her and will definitely recommend her to others."

After reading the students' kind feedback, I knew my dark days of trouble had ended. I started learning to relax and enjoy my new profession, for I finally understood I could positively impact the industry I loved by helping to produce professionals who could critically think, take perspective, cared about quality, safety, and, most of all, the well-being of the people they would have the honor to lead. In 2014, I was offered a full-time position. Two years later, I was invited to engage in the tenure process, a challenge I accepted with gratitude.

I now long for all professors to experience not just the same but higher levels of success in authentic learning. Over the course of my teaching, I have concluded, learning should always include the *how* and the *why*. It must provide both purpose and meaning so it can inspire the learner to think freely and creatively about the content.

Unfortunately, that is not how most learning environments are created. We are too focused on grades and thus have relied on passive learning because of its efficiency in relating concepts and knowledge. Passive learning holds the student responsible for content acquisition of the *how* but does very little to explain *why* and *how* all of these concepts interconnect to form a larger perspective. I believe students must learn the facts, but the facts must always be accompanied with a rich context of problems and questions that allow them to build on previously gained information. Questions feed curiosity, and curiosity provides the basis of scholarly work. It sustains and feeds our desire to discover new knowledge.

Some professors have shared with me that although they do want to incorporate more creative work in the classroom, they feel as if they cannot because activities take time, hindering the professor's ability to cover a significant amount of content. Additionally, the tenure process places scholarly requirements on professors, focusing their efforts on the production of research and scholarly activity rather than the development of innovative ways to teach content. I do understand and sometimes struggle to find the balance. However, I believe by skillfully incorporating educational games into our lectures, we are able to carefully apply more quality to the content versus just quantity of content.

In summary, I have found adding educational activities and stories has provided more value to my teaching. It is not always easy to find games that fit well with the classroom, but the search is often worth it. At the end of this book, you will find a collection of basic, ready-to-use examples you can manipulate to begin moving toward a more active, visual presentation of some material as a way to complement your rich lectures. Student participation is excellent, particularly as students become more comfortable with an active learning classroom environment. I enjoy teaching this way because the students seem liberated to ask questions and feel moved to speak without my constant encouragement.

CHAPTER 2

WHY SHOULD WE BE TEACHING DIFFERENTLY?

"Too often we give children answers to remember rather than problems to solve"

ROGER LEWIN

"Your research proposal is quite good...but it is not dissertation worthy yet." This would be the second time Dr. Kennedy, my dissertation chair, would utter such devastating words during our monthly status report call. After offering additional explanation, the call ended with me promising to do more to bring my proposal into clearer focus. I hung up the phone and began thinking perhaps, this was too difficult of an endeavor for me. Maybe I was simply not good enough to be a scholar. I stood up and opened my office door ready to face what seemed simpler: being a hospital administrator in charge of the day-to-day operations of 150 medical beds, an outpatient clinic, over 250 employees, ten physicians, and a fifteen-million-dollar budget. As I walked out of my office, Linda, my secretary, had a cup of coffee ready for me.

I remember saying, "I just fear I am not good enough and I will never be able to finish it."

Linda wisely responded, "I am not sure why you are letting this get the best of you. You cannot quit, you must continue… don't you know you have inspired me and so many others to pursue our college education? You cannot give up."

For the rest of the afternoon and evening, I kept thinking about Linda's comments. But how could I ever produce such a research proposal? I had already spent over a hundred hours creating two unsuccessful proposals. What could I do differently? The following morning, as I drove into work, I began thinking about a time I had a similar experience. It was during my undergraduate studies. I was taking a research course with Dr. Bruce Darby, professor of psychology at Florida Southern College. At that time, I remember meeting with him to discuss my research idea and after some discussion, I was able to clearly articulate and outline the research objectives. Ultimately, my research work exceeded expectations and Dr. Darby challenged me to submit it for consideration to a national research conference. A few weeks later, I received notification that my research study had been selected and I was to present it in New Orleans. I was excited for the opportunity, yet terrified, as it meant I would have to get to the conference on my own. I had never driven to any place that took longer than an hour to get there before and flying was simply not in my mother's budget. She already had three jobs to get my brother and me through college. When I shared the predicament with my mother, she quickly explained, if my professors believed in me, she would support me. She requested three days off from her three jobs and off we went. Not only was I able to present my research, but I also received a student research award. *So, how could I do it then and not now?* I recalled.

As soon as I arrived at my office, I called Dr. Darby. I hoped he would still remember me even though ten years had passed since graduation. Much to my surprise, not only did he remember my performance in his class and at the national conference, but he also shared my picture from the national research convention was still in the professors' conference room. He also shared he and my other professors, Dr. Weaver, Dr. Mugg, and Dr. Ivey, often sat and reminisced about past students' success with new students. I was humbled and surprised they all remembered me as if I was a member of a closed knit family. The class size was and remains between twenty to twenty-five students per classroom, allowing professors to have a more authentic relationship with each of their students.

A few days later, I found myself back in an undergraduate classroom, writing all over the board, explaining my research vision to Dr. Darby, who listened carefully and intently. Before I knew it, our conversation led me directly into the clarity of thought I so desperately sought. I went back and wrote purposefully once again. Three months later, Dr. Kennedy accepted my research proposal. My dissertation defense was flawless and my research served as a model for assessing access to preventative health.

We all need professors like Dr. Darby and Dr. Kennedy—professors who can see the potential in their students and who recognize the importance of challenging them to critically think and solve problems. However, it seems that finding professors who know their students well enough to change them is difficult, especially at large colleges and universities where introductory level courses are held in lecture halls with 150 to 300 students in a class. These large enrollment classes rely on fact-oriented, instructor-centered, lecture-based instruction, which can hinder the students' ability to develop and practice critical thinking skills. Contrast such student experience with your own college experience and how you were able to call up a professor ten years later and talk through another research project with him.

Last Thanksgiving dinner, I was fortunate to have several of my children's childhood friends around the table. We all sat around while they remembered people, teachers, and funny stories about growing up in our neighborhood. They all started to share stories about their college experiences. Many of them attended mid to large sized colleges and universities across the United States. They talked about what it was like being a number in the hundreds of students in a lecture hall. Much to my surprise, they all shared how wonderful it was to be able to hide among the crowd. Then, suddenly, the conversation took a turn. They all started complaining about having to teach themselves most of the concepts being taught in class because there were just too many students in the course. They all shared the best way to pass large enrollment courses was to simply memorize and regurgitate information during exam time.

When I asked about actually learning concepts to later use in higher-level courses, they simply said, "Well, we will just memorize some more...it's working. We are all passing."

Unbeknownst to them, what they were describing is referred to as rote learning, which is indeed an incredibly useful knowledge building block. For example, you cannot do chemistry efficiently without having the Table of Elements memorized and you cannot be effective at algebra without memorizing the basic rules and properties of algebra first. According to board certified neurologist and classroom teacher Dr. Judy Willis, "Rote memorization doesn't work for students because there is no engaging pattern or effort made to relate the content to students' lives. Another problem is that short term memory can only hold data for 20 minutes" (Willis, 2007). What is important to note is without rote memorization, we probably would not be as likely to have "ah-ha" moments or breakthroughs. In other words, rote learning should be a means to an end, not an end itself.

From a pedagogical perspective, as faculty, we must develop learning goals at multiple cognitive levels and corresponding classroom activities to support the development of a broad range of cognitive skills. Additionally, assessments must be able to test beyond lower cognitive processes (i.e., recalling and comprehending facts) as they do not prepare students to transfer, connect, nor apply knowledge to realistic problem solving (Bransford et al., 1999, Handelsman et al., 2007). Handelsman et al. further explain the changes needed to transform the classroom to leverage higher level thinking are not as great as most might imagine. They argue the principles and skills scientists use to guide their work in their laboratories are the same ones needed to guide their activities in their classrooms.

We must also recognize we have been living in a world where each one of us carries along with our mobile device a built-in, voice-controlled personal assistant that is constantly growing in its intelligence and abilities. Our personal devices can solve problems, process information, and answer questions in a matter of seconds. In essence, we live in a world where artificial intelligence has made it easy for us to quickly inquire about any fact and figure ever known to humankind. Since we live in this artificial intelligence environment where information is so accessible, why is it that our higher education system continues to rely on having students memorize facts and figures?

Recently, I witnessed a student getting ready for a marketing exam. As I walked closer to where she was, I noticed her whispering the words to herself repeatedly making sure the words settled inside her memory bank.

I was curious and I asked, "How is it going?"

She answered proudly, "Fine, Dr. Falcon, I have spent all night memorizing all of the definitions so I should be golden." I walked away deflated, knowing that in a matter of days, if not just hours, most of that knowledge would be forgotten. Besides, all of those definitions can be provided by artificial intelligence in a matter of seconds. Our ability to connect all of those data points to come to a new understanding is the key to our education and our own journey into new discoveries. So, why are we not reframing the system of education based on where the world is going instead of continuing to do the same thing over and over again?

I do agree, some things are worth memorizing such as addresses, PINs, and birthdays. The definition of market segmentation is not among them. It is a fact that matters only insofar as it connects to other ideas and its importance to the success of a business. To learn it in isolation is meaningless. It is a way of knowing without learning, of answering without understanding. Memorization is not all harmful, however. I believe it is a healthy part of a balanced scholastic diet, as knowledge matters. A head full of facts, even memorized facts, is better than an empty one. In addition, factual knowledge is needed, as it provides the basis from which to learn to reason critically. However, we must remember, memorized knowledge is not half as useful as knowledge that is actually understood.

Overreliance on memorization is like most problems in education, systemic. It is also fueled by its reliance on multiple choice testing. As professors, we have access to "test banks" supplied by textbook publishers as part of the textbook resources. Professors sometimes use these test banks to devise their own tests. Often, the "test bank" questions are designed, catering to the classic testing model: rote memorization with a high-stakes, time-pressured, single unit, in-class exam. In our syllabi, we include when students can expect to be tested so it is easy for students to carve out the night before to cram.

Additionally, students and professors alike know there are too many tests to grade, so the easier route is to ask quick-to-correct factual and computational questions using a Scantron for grading, exactly the type where memorization mostly pays off. In order to diminish this dependency on memorization, some professors have allowed students a cheat sheet page of notes during tests; however, unless the test questions demand a high level of thought, you are left with the worst of both worlds, a test that requires neither deep understanding nor basic factual knowledge.

To make matters worse, a new threat has been uncovered. Back in 2010, a cheating scandal was discovered at the University of Central Florida (UCF). Administrators explained, senior-level business students purchased a test bank for their class' textbook, which was shared with about two hundred classmates. Assuming the "test bank" was secured, a professor used the same three-hundred-question test bank to create his midterm exam. The outcomes were unusually high grades along with national news media coverage of the cheating scandal.

Fast forward a few years, students can use websites that provide instant answers to any homework question with the help of artificial intelligence. Apps, such as Socratic by Google, Course Hero, and Chegg, to name a few, provide answers to a student's homework problems in a matter of seconds. Some of these apps also offer a photo-based solution search. By taking a picture of their homework or test problem, students receive an answer formulated by qualified academics, as well as any work involved in finding the solution (Socratic.org, Coursehero.com, Chegg.com). The use of these apps for graded assignments would violate almost every school's honor code.

Notwithstanding, the UCF incident along with newer homework help technology, have brought about debates regarding academic integrity and the readily availability of test banks and homework answers to students focused solely on course grades. We need to teach students real knowledge and test them on that knowledge in a way where they can't cheat by asking them questions that require critical thinking. And, we need to facilitate school environments that make that possible for professors.

Our current education system is producing robots that can regurgitate information, but what we really need to cultivate is the kind of thinking that computers cannot do (yet): discovering new facts about our universe, coming up with new ideas that have not been explored before, etc. In a world of fast-advancing artificial intelligence, robotics, and the Fourth Industrial Revolution, we must prepare students for uncertainty and promote agility and adaptability. Students need to "learn how to learn" and how to critically think in order to solve problems. These are the skills not provided by artificial intelligence—these are unique human skills that can be taught and learned.

Arguably, one of the best indicators of our work as educators is having employers at our schools' doorsteps ready and eager to hire our students. The 2020 Global University Employability Survey spotlights a potentially transformative trend. Of the surveyed participants, 28 percent believe the purpose of university is to produce "ready-to-work" graduates, up from just 8 percent a decade ago. The survey gathers responses from almost nine thousand graduate recruiters worldwide on a series of issues, including their views on the top universities for employability. The trend toward firms emphasizing graduate employability provides a good opportunity for professors to completely reimagine their pedagogy and for universities to create an environment to support such initiatives.

So, what is a "ready-to-work" graduate? According to an online survey conducted by Morning Consult, employers want college graduates who have "soft skills," such as being a good listener or thinking critically, but they have difficulty finding such candidates (Cengage, 2019). The survey included respondents from more than five hundred hiring managers, more than 150 human resources professionals, and more than 1,500 current and former college students from two- and four-year institutions. The companies found the most in-demand talent among employers was listening skills—74 percent of employers indicated this was a skill they valued. This was followed by attention to detail (70 percent), and effective communication (69 percent). About 73 percent of the employers said, finding qualified candidates was somewhat or very difficult. Roughly one-third of the employers (34 percent) indicated colleges and universities have not prepared students for jobs. The students reported finding jobs was challenging. About 77 percent also expressed concerns about whether they had the skills needed for a job.

Offering additional support to this claim, the National Association of Colleges and Employers (NACE), recommends college students provide evidence to potential employers of their problem solving skills and teamwork abilities on their resumes. Their recommendation is backed by NACE's Job Outlook 2020 survey, which found that beyond a relevant major for the position and a strong GPA, problem solving skills and the ability to work as part of a team are the attributes employers most want to see on resumes. Ninety-one percent of employer respondents are seeking signs of a candidate's problem solving skills, and 86 percent want proof of a candidate's ability to work as part of a team. These attributes, albeit in different order of importance, were also among the most wanted attributes in 2019. Other top attributes this year are a strong work ethic, analytical/quantitative skills, written communication skills, leadership, and verbal communication skills.

A fairly easy and inexpensive method faculty have utilized to bridge the gap has been inviting professionals into the classroom to teach and speak about current problems they are facing. While academics have an in depth knowledge of the theories and their field of expertise, industry professionals tend to have more comprehensive knowledge of the inner workings of the professional world, including the markets, systems, and processes. Having experienced and distinguished specialists teach in an academic setting is an excellent way to have students connect the material to current problems and situations being faced by professionals in the field, thus creating meaningful and robust learning experiences. If you do not know where to start or simply run out of viable connections, there is a simple solution. Neprics.com exists to connect industry leaders to classrooms virtually. This is their mission, and it should be yours too.

CHAPTER 3

WHAT THE BEST TEACHERS ARE DOING

"If you want to build a ship, don't drum up people to collect wood and don't assign them tasks and work, but rather teach them to long for the endless immensity of the sea"

ANTOINE DE SAINT-EXUPERY

When our then-provost, Dr. Kyle Fedler, welcomed us as the newly hired faculty cohort, he spoke of the teaching profession similar to the parable of the scattering seed where we don't know if, how, and where the seeds we scatter will take root. He explained that sometimes, our work bears fruit in ways we can't even imagine. This is what he called "the ministry of teaching." Dr. Fedler provided each of us with a book titled *What The Best College Teachers Do,* by Ken Bain and published in 2004. He challenged us to read it so we could become the best scatterers of seeds.

I took Dr. Fedler's advice to heart. I devoured the book in a matter of hours. One of the first takeaways from the book was learning that exceptional teachers work backwards. They start with the end in mind. They start by first outlining the key concepts they want their students to understand, evaluate, and analyze by the end of the course. In other words, they develop the courses for students to sequentially experience and learn what it means to think like an accountant, a manager, a historian, and a biologist, weaving into their lectures the concepts central to their discipline. Second, they believe in their students' ability to perform and convey such trust by inviting them to be active participants in their learning. In other words, the students should be doing the heavy lifting.

Bain illustrated this last concept by sharing Dr. Sandel's teaching philosophy. As a well-respected and highly sought Harvard professor, Dr. Sandel compares teaching in higher education to teaching a child how to play baseball. "You would never consider providing a child detailed step by step instructions on how to swing the bat, where to stand, the rules of the game or you could simply give them the bat and let her swing. Learning the basics of swinging using what has already been acquired: balance, eye movement, and coordination." In other words, using the knowledge that has been gained and build upon it.

Armed with the new knowledge gained from Bain's book, I began where I suspect most new to academics begin: a meeting with an appointed mentor who would introduce me to the school's learning management system (LMS), the textbook being used by other professors teaching the class, and a sample of their syllabi. My mentor proceeded to guide me as to where and how to download the professor's resources available from the publisher's website, which included PowerPoints and question banks for each chapter. An emphasis was placed for me to cover all of the chapters, as "covering more is always better."

As I thought deeply about the pathway set in front of me, I realized a big gap existed between what I learned from Bain's book, the passive learning, and lecture based approach using PowerPoints, and content that was already curated by a publisher at least a year ago. I recall walking away from the meeting thinking this traditional method of teaching would get the work done, but at the expense of every single one of my students' learning.

Since the first semester of teaching, I've resolved to follow prophet Mahatma Gandhi's challenge to be the change I wished to see in the world. I wanted to develop a classroom environment where students would be actively engaged in their learning. I wanted my students to want to come to class because they enjoyed learning and not because they had to do so for the attendance points. I knew I could learn to be a better teacher and in doing so, I might, perhaps, positively influence the course of their lives. I resolved to be an inspirational teacher. I began to gather tips from my own experience, from peers, students, and pedagogical experts on how to create an inviting learning environment and promote student success. Below, you will find a listing of those tips and ideas.

CREATE AN INVITING LEARNING ENVIRONMENT:

As professors, we intuitively understand the need to create a welcoming community in their classrooms. A warm and responsive classroom culture is essential because, like all of us, students need to feel safe and valued in order to thrive. Dr. Melissa Garr, assistant professor of modern languages at Florida Southern College, establishes this concept simply and eloquently by using a metaphor. She shares early in the semester that her class is like a "Spanish bounce house meaning this is a space to take linguistic risks and 'jump' as high as they can because 'failing down: (making mistakes) won't hurt here.'" She further explains, no one is allowed to make fun of one another because she is the only one who is qualified to do so, and that is simply not her job. She further explains, it is important for them to "practice bouncing in the bouncy house so that when they leave it and go out in to the real world, they either do not make mistakes, or if they do, it won't 'hurt' as badly." Dr. Garr emphasizes this concept throughout the semester by allowing students to rewrite drafts of compositions through self and peer correction.

BUILD COMMUNITY AND SET A POSITIVE TONE:

To establish a similar sense of connection among college students is difficult and requires some creative thinking. Dr. Kira Omelchenko, associate professor of music and conductor of the Laurier Symphony Orchestra, explains, "it is important to allow students to connect with one another to build a strong sense of community. It is not just us and the students." She explains, it is important to set the classroom experience from the moment the students walk into the classroom space. In doing so, she typically asks students to share the good news of the day. which only takes five minutes of class time. This practice allows students not just to share their successes or events coming up with one another, but to celebrate as a community. Here are some additional tips on how you can build community:

- Learn your students' names as quickly as possible. Most learning management systems allow students to upload their pictures. If this is the case at your institution, try to learn their faces and their names before the semester begins. This will allow you to have an early start to memorizing their names. You can also start the semester by playing a game (see icebreaker suggestions within this book) and/or by having them provide information on an index card such as:

  - The reasons why they enrolled in the course (if an elective).
  - What are they most looking forward to learning?
  - What are some topics they would like to learn about that are not listed on the syllabus?
  - What are their goals after graduation and how will this course help them achieve their goals?
  - What is their favorite song, movie, or meme?

- Keep using index cards at the beginning of the semester and collect them at the end of each class. This will allow you to efficiently and accurately take attendance without taking time from class.
- Play music before class begins. Create a playlist from their favorite songs and artists. Include some of yours as well. Purposefully play the clean versions of the songs the students identified as their favorites. Doing so allows you to create a fun space ahead of the class session.
- Setting the rules of engagement early is of the utmost importance in both building community and setting a positive tone. For example, if late assignments are not

accepted or extra credit assignments are not provided, share this information early and often so students know and (hopefully) minimize student emails.

- Arrive to class a few minutes early, engage students in conversation, and greet students as they enter the classroom.
- Start with an agenda for the class session. Use it to orient students as to what will be happening in the class session as well as provide reminders of upcoming assignments and due dates.
- Do not set up meetings or office hours that end right before your class is set to start. Resist the temptation to do so. Make sure to allow yourself ten to fifteen minutes before class just to focus, update the agenda for the day, and gather your energy.
- If it is a large on-line class made up of various student undergraduate levels (e.g., freshman, sophomores, juniors, seniors), set up ten to fifteen minutes at the onset of class via breakout rooms and meet individually with students from each level. They tend to have different questions and needs.
- Be mindful that everyone needs a "seventh inning stretch." If you have to drive content through a longer lecture, provide students with a five-minute stretch and hydrate moment, especially if you have students who have classes back to back. Remember, those students only have ten to fifteen minutes of active movement in between classes.
- Lose the podium. Wander around. Dr. Roberto, Bryant University professor and author of *Unlocking Creativity,* says, the podium is a physical and psychological barrier for engagement. If you must, use index cards to serve as a guide to help you meet your class objectives.

- "Add some coffee hours to your office hours," says Dr. Omelchenko. "If you are going to meet with students, why not meet them at the school's coffee shop instead?" Doing so breaks up the monotony and allows students to feel more comfortable being in a neutral environment.
- Smile. Just the simple act of putting a smile on your face can lead you to feel actual happiness, joy, or amusement.

PROMOTE STUDENT SUCCESS:

What we believe about our students and their potential matters to their level of motivation, engagement, grades, and learning. Bain found a similar pattern while conducting his research (Bain, 2004). In the book, Bain wrote, "the key to understanding the best teaching can be found not in particular practices or rules, but in the *attitude* of the teachers, in their faith in their students' ability to achieve, in their willingness to take their students' seriously, and...from mutual respect and agreement between students and teachers." Here are a few ideas that can help promote a more positive attitude:

- Engage previous learning at the onset of class. Start class by asking for three things they remember from the previous class session to help you assess what students know and what they may be missing as a formative and summative assessment strategy. These can be facts, figures, or new assumptions they made. For example:
    - Dr. Barbi Honeycutt, author, educator and podcaster, introduces the 3-2-1 strategy in her blog, *Lecture Breakers*. It can be introduced at the beginning of a class session, before class based on a pre-reading assignment, and after student presentations. In this formative assessment technique, students are asked three

simple questions at the end of class: 1) What are the three things they learned, 2) What are two things that confirmed what they already know, and lastly, 3) What is one question they still have. Dr. Honeycutt explains this strategy provides several benefits among which are decreasing frustration (Lecture breakers, 2021).

  - Dr. Claire Howel Major, professor of higher education administration at the University of Alabama, asks students at the beginning of class to write a note to an imaginary classmate who missed the last class, summarizing what was covered. This helps them recall and synthesize information and primes them to learn (Lecture breakers, 2021).

- Give all students an opportunity to use their voice. At the beginning of the semester, you will typically have only a couple of hands go up. Do call upon those students who volunteer, but also call upon a person whose hand did not go up. This practice will allow you to hear everyone's voice. By a few class sessions, all students will know they have to be ready with an answer reinforcing the expectation of commitment and accountability. The exercise will allow you to watch the student's reactions, read body language, and ask additional questions prompting spontaneous exchange, which primes them to be active for the new material.
- Emphasize the importance of errors in learning. For example, Dr. Garr often reminds students that she does not expect perfection, and in doing so, she has found that students tend to then stop the use of internet translations

for Spanish language compositions because they are no longer under the false belief that mistakes mean failure.

- Develop detailed and clear rubrics for each of your assignments. Rubrics provide a guide for students to better understand expectations and motivate self-assessment. They also help establish a common ground, making the grading process more transparent.
- Take a "temperature test" mid semester. Mid semester course evaluations are a great opportunity to gather students' opinions as to how class is going and what might be improved over the rest of the semester. The empirical evidence suggests that not only will you be able to gather valuable information about what is working for them and what have been some of the barriers or struggles to their learning, but it will also likely enhance your course evaluation rate of return at the end of the semester. Some suggestions of questions to ask are: (1) Which aspect of the course is most helpful to you? (2) Which aspect of the course is least helpful to you? (3) Are there any suggestions you would like to make about how to improve the course? You could also ask: (1) What can I keep on doing to help you learn the most in this class? (2) What concepts, if any, have you struggled the most and why? You can ask these questions anonymously via index cards or you can create a zero-point assignment within your learning management system.
- Make a point to know what the students care about and what apps they use; stay relevant and bring examples that align with such topics. Students will lean forward because it matters to them.

- Use songs, mnemonic devices, and formulas to make content easy to remember. For example, Dr. Omelchenko helps students memorize Bach's Brandenburg Concept No. 3 in G by having students sing along to the music as follows: "Brandenburg No. 3...Brandenburg it's in G...Brandenburg it's by Bach and has a lot of strings and things..."

SIMPLIFY THE COMPLICATED

I met Professor Jozsi on my first day of the academic orientation as we sat next to each other by pure coincidence. From our initial exchange, I learned Professor Jozsi came to our school having served thirty-five successful years at another school and while there, she had earned twenty teaching awards. When I asked what made her teaching so successful, she said, "It's simple...I boil everything down to three simple steps with visuals. I develop one handout that covers the content of one full chapter." Professor Jozsi insists the goal is not to impress students with our knowledge, but rather, to simplify what we know to help them acquire new knowledge. She explains, we must "begin with simple generalizations using familiar language and then slowly and gradually move towards complexity and specificity." Here are some ideas that will help you explain complicated things in a simple way:

- Start by holding the students' attention by leveraging what the student already knows, or think they know. Use what is important to them. Practice what telemarketers know best, which is to "never feed salad to a lion" (Acunzo, 2018). Put your students' needs first. Sometimes you have to go back in order to go forward. Review foundational knowledge before gradually, yet systematically, you move them into the new concept and idea.

- Show and tell them the why behind the need to know the material. Use YouTube, streaming videos, podcasts, and news feeds to help you bring the material to life and gain the students' interest.
- Identify the top three messages or concepts you want them to learn during the class session. Choose quality over quantity.
- Be creative. Look for ways to bring your material to life in a fun, interesting manner. For example:
  - "A Muggle's Guide to Harry Potter's Chemistry" is a class offered by Dr. Rebecca Lai, assistant professor at the University of Nebraska-Lincoln. She developed the class to entice non-chemistry majors to learn more about chemistry and science. In the class, students learn how "a shrinking potion could be connected to reverse-aging chemicals like antioxidants." The class has been so popular that the capacity had to be increased to allow additional students in the course. Since the class runs through Halloween, students are allowed to dress up as if they were in Hogwarts (Jones, 2011).
  - Dr. Deborah Bromfield-Lee, associate professor of chemistry at Florida Southern College, offers a class titled "Chemistry of Food and Cooking." Students learn the physical and chemical changes associated with food preparation and storage (FSC Academic Catalog, 2019).

DO LECTURE AND DO PLAY

I think we would all agree that as professors, we love imparting knowledge and inspiring change. We value diversity of perspectives and experiences that enrich our understanding of an issue; we have a lot to learn by sitting down and simply talking to one another. At several junctions of our lives' journeys, we have often swum against the prevailing tides in search for clarity and deeper meaning. We love to share what we know and the excitement of what we have yet to know through the old and well-established tradition of lectures.

Lectures allow us the opportunity to have students figure out the significance and the interrelatedness of all the materials taught in the course. In recent years, however, teaching using a lecture format has been under attack. In fact, an analysis of research studies by Freeman et. al. published in 2014, found that "active learning leads to increases in examination performance that would raise average grades by a half a letter, and that failure rates under traditional lecturing increased by 55 percent over the rates observed under active learning" (Freeman et. al., 2014). So, why are we still lecturing in higher education? Perhaps, because creating an environment that promotes meaningful learning is hard and it takes time. We are already under pressure for time. Many of us find it extraordinarily difficult to keep up with work demands and family responsibilities. I could add more statistics here, but the truth of the matter is I do not think I have to convince you. However, should you want to feel corroborated, I invite you to read, *The Faculty Time Divide, by Jerry Jacobs* (Jacobs, 2004). His main point, we work too hard.

So, assuming we had some time, should we drop everything and use active learning all the time? Donald Finkel, the author of a book titled, *Teaching with Your Mouth Shut*, does not say that teachers ought *never* to talk. Lecturing has some role to play when the goal is just to transmit knowledge—at least when that knowledge cannot be discovered (or simply read) by the students. Most importantly, lectures allow us the opportunity to break down students' preconceptions and beliefs by providing scientific evidence to further inform what they know or help them change their beliefs (Confrey, 1990; Minstrell, 1989). For example, consider Lionni's (1970) tale titled *Fish is Fish*. In it, the author describes a fish and a tadpole who are the best of friends. The tadpole develops into a frog and eventually leaves the pond. The frog friend returns to the pond a few weeks later and recants vivid stories about his extraordinary experiences on land. The frog describes things like birds, cows, and people. As the fish is being told these stories, he begins to imagine what they are like. Each starts as a fish-like form adapted to accommodate the traits being described by the frog. For example, people are imagined to be fish who walk on their tailfins, birds are fish with wings, cows are fish with udders.

Fish is Fish is a perfect yet simple analogy to describe what happens when new knowledge is built without addressing and clarifying existing knowledge. Thus, lectures allow us to confront head-on the foundational knowledge the student brings, rebuild that foundation, or fill in the gaps if necessary, and move them to a more mature understanding of the subject matter.

Dr. Claire Howell Major, a professor of higher education administration at the University of Alabama, is also here to tell us that lecturing is fine. I think that is worth repeating. Lecturing is fine. In fact, she argues, it is often crucial to a successful class. The key, says Major, during a *Lecture Breakers* podcast with Dr. Barbi Honeycutt, is to make the lecture interactive. Here is a collection of some basic ideas about lectures and play:

- Shamelessly lecture, but do so intentionally and creatively. For example, Dr. Major uses lectures as bookends to begin and end class. Use the common think-pair-share exercise in between lecture time to gather students in small groups to work individually and share their answers. A small work group encourages them to practice what they just learned and reframe information. Simon Sinek, author and inspirational speaker, explains, "if you make something simple, it's repeatable. If the information is repeatable, it's understandable and the best part about that is others then can share your thinking (teachings) without you" (Sinek 2014).
- Lecture with guided notes. Students are given a handout summarizing key points in the lecture, but with blank spaces that they need to fill in as they go along.
- Provide or ask for a real-world application of a point made during the lecture.
- Use a lecture wrapper. Ask students to summarize the most important points of the lecture as well as those they found most confusing, then review those summaries together.
- If there is a body of knowledge students must master, provide more of it in readings between class sessions or include time for students to complete short readings during class sessions. Add time for discussion to skillfully pull from the lecture the concepts you are trying to teach.

- Don't spoil the lecture by adding every point to the PowerPoint. If it is written, students will get ahead and stop engaging.
- Don't be a slave to the textbook. It is simply a guide. You are the expert and the one that ultimately determines what, when, and how the material gets covered.

RE-THINKING ASSESSMENT:

As an academic, I have witnessed our reliance on multiple choice tests because, as I have learned, scoring is quick and easy, often delivered and automatically graded via a learning management system, and can be graded without rater bias, among many other positive features. However, the biggest problem I have found with multiple choice questions is that a student can potentially obtain a right answer by guessing instead of really knowing the content. As a matter of fact, the right answer is right in front of them.

Kathrin Stanger-Hall (2017) set out to test the effect of exam format on students' critical thinking skills by using two sections of an introductory biology class. One section was assessed using traditional multiple choice questions while the second section was assessed using a mixture of multiple choice and constructed response questions. The results of the study indicated that introducing constructed response questions encouraged students to learn more and become better critical thinkers and reduced gender bias. The results suggest the multiple choice only exam format "hinders critical thinking in introductory science classes."

So, if we are spending a tremendous amount of energy and time on reconfiguring our teaching so students become effective critical thinkers, why do we waste all that effort by using multiple choice questions, which allow guessing, promote rote learning, and provide no opportunity for students to synthesize, analyze, and create ideas? If this was a multiple choice question, the answer, I would guess, is because we have always done it this way.

Bestselling author and organizational psychologist, Adam Grant, challenges us through his 2021 book, *Think Again,* to embrace the joy of being wrong. Grant provides an example we probably have all heard before from political speeches. The boiling frog fable goes something like this: if you put a frog into a pot of boiling water, it will jump right out. But, if you put it in a pot of nice comfortable water and then turn on the heat, the frog will not realize the magnitude of the problem until it is too late. Grant conducted some research on this fable and he found it to be false! While the frog thrown in the boiling water may or may not jump out, the one in the gradually heating water will jump out the minute the water becomes too hot. Adam writes, "It's not the frogs who fail to re-evaluate. It is us. Once we hear the story, we accept it as true, we rarely bother to question it."

The good news is that in recent years, a coalition of education leaders, employers, researchers, and policymakers are joining forces, looking to reform assessment. Dr. Bill Lucas, professor of learning and director of the Centre for Real-World Learning at the University of Winchester in the UK, argues that current approaches to assessment use "the wrong kinds of nets," especially if we are wanting to "catch" young people's strengths. In April of 2021, Dr. Lucas published an article titled, "Rethinking Assessment in Education: The Case for Change," in which he examines worldwide innovative practices in assessment. Bill Lucas explains a relatively new model reframing the contemporary curriculum and moving away from the 3Rs of education (Reading, wRiting, and aRithmetic) to focus more on what twenty-first-century learners need most: confidence, curiosity, collaboration, creativity, commitment and craftmanship (Claxton & Lucas, 2015). Other variants include the one adopted by Deeper Learning (Character, Citizenship, Collaboration, Communication, Creativity and Critical Thinking) (Claxton & Lucas 2015).

While Bill Lucas provides evidence that the curriculum is changing worldwide to incorporate the new variants, assessment has been left behind. There are many aspects of educational assessment today that are failing according to Lucas, and they fall into four categories: "1) what is assessed (focus); 2) how it is assessed (methods); 3) the impact of the assessment process (consequences); and the uses made of the assessment (validity)." Complex, higher order skills are rarely assessed in ways that recognize the subtleties involved. Many dispositions or capabilities known to be important in life are not assessed at all (Lucas, 2021).

Let us pick up the battle. We can stop being slaves to the textbook and to the test banks. Let us determine what is important to assess and do so in such a way that measures knowledge and deductive and inductive reasoning, which are increasingly important for our global economy and fast-changing world.

CHAPTER 4

WHY STORYTELLING IS MAGICAL AND KEY TO LECTURES

"Good stories surprise us. They make us think and feel. They stick in our minds and help us remember ideas and concepts in a way that a PowerPoint crammed with bar graphs never can."

JOE LAZAUSKAS AND SHANE SNOW, THE STORYTELLING EDGE

I learned from listening to Neil Gaiman, one of the most prolific storytellers of our time, that stories are magical because there are so many emotions packed inside of them, but it is the listener who pulls them out. Allow me to share a story:

When I finally understood that leadership was about seeing the potential in others and raising them up so they could achieve greatness, I began auditing my life looking for those leaders who so graciously and selflessly invested in me. As I dove deeper into my life, I realized that in over thirty years, I had only encountered a couple of great leaders who had encouraged me to look inside myself and believe in the beauty of my God-given purpose. Thanks to their narrative and efforts, I was able to let go of the many instances I was told I was not good enough.

You see, I remember being about six or seven years old, glancing out of a large airport window and waiting for some family members to arrive. It was the first time I had ever been to an airport, so I was completely taken by the new environment. The plane landed and, as in most Mexican province airports, the passengers de-boarded by coming down via a mobile escalator. My dad came and stood right beside me and pointed and waved to the family members who smiled and waved back in excitement. As the last of the passengers walked down the escalator, I noticed a couple of people in uniform staying back. I remember looking up at that point and asking my dad who they were.

"Those are the flight attendants and the pilot," he explained. My mind raced and I began to imagine their lives traveling from place to place, meeting new people and seeing the world.

Not even thinking, my mouth said, "I want be a pilot when I grow up."

My dad took a step closer to me and said, "Well, let's think about that...they do travel all over the world and probably lead amazing lives, but you're a girl and there are not many girl pilots. Plus, how would take care of your family if you are always gone? And you have to be pretty smart to become a pilot." The conversation ended as soon as everyone started hugging and welcoming the family. The thought of becoming a pilot never crossed my mind again.

Fast forward five years, we found ourselves surrounding my grandmother's hospital bed. She was holding my hand tightly as if she knew I would not see her alive again. A lady in a white lab coat entered the hospital room and acknowledged the family. She introduced herself as my grandmother's attending physician, and made her way to my grandmother's side, and held her hand in a genuine gesture of compassion. After some small talk, my parents asked my brother and I to leave the room so they could discuss the plan of care with the doctor. As I stood outside of the hospital room, I remember being impressed by the physician's confidence and professional demeanor. I liked how she took command of the room and showed her kindness and support for her patient.

About an hour later, my parents came out of the hospital room and explained that my grandmother would undergo surgery that afternoon. We went to the hospital's cafeteria, where I saw more doctors and nurses going about their day. As we waited for my grandmother to come out of surgery, I shared with my dad how impressed I was with my grandmother's physician. I shared with him that I wanted to become a doctor and help patients and their families in the darkest of times.

Unapologetically, he said, "You know, it is really nice that you want to be a doctor. They do make a lot of money, but they are slaves to their profession. They have to be very smart." And, as if that was not enough, he added, "You're going to get married and have a family. You cannot let your profession get in the way of being a wife and a mother. Plus, it really requires a lot of intelligence, and you don't have any of that...your brother does, if he wanted to be a physician, I'm pretty sure he could."

So I went on living my life with its unexpected twists and turns, one of which involved my parents separating. My dad left and would not come into my life again for another twenty years. I was in my mid-thirties by then. When he came to visit, I was already married and had two young boys. I had also completed two master's degrees and was about to defend my doctoral dissertation proposal. I had become a successful healthcare professional thanks to many mentors who not only saw potential in me, but also gave me opportunities to grow personally and professionally. By this time, I had already started climbing up the corporate ladder. I was in charge of several hospital units, over ten physicians, and an outpatient clinic. All in all, I was responsible for the lives of over 250 people and a twenty-million-dollar budget.

While my dad was visiting, I was called in to work to take care of a situation. I told my dad I had to leave for a few hours, but I would return that afternoon to take him out to dinner. To my surprise, he asked if he could come along as he wanted to spend as much time as possible with me before he left. I agreed. As we walked into the hospital, I was greeted with a smile by just about every person we encountered. I stopped and talked with a couple of physicians as my dad made himself comfortable in one of the unit's waiting rooms. Eventually, we made it to my office. One of my assistants was already waiting for me with coffee, which I appreciated immensely, given my fast-paced work environment. I introduced her to my dad and then we walked into my office so that I could leave him there and address the situation at hand.

"This is a very nice office," he said. "You must be the head of all secretaries here. You have done well for yourself."

I looked at him and said calmly and respectfully, "You know...I am not sure what I would do without my assistant, she is just wonderful. I am so thankful to be her leader so I can support her and help her grow personally and professionally. But, you're mistaken—I am actually a Director of Clinical Services at this hospital, and every person you encountered on our way to this office reports to me, including the physicians."

I believe it was the first time my dad was speechless. He truly did not know what to say. I told him to feel at ease and that I would be back in a couple of hours, at most. As I walked away from my dad, I was engulfed with an overwhelming feeling of gratefulness. Yes, gratefulness. I thought about the many professors who saw my potential and of the many leaders who used their position of influence to positively affect my thoughts and my actions. It took a lot of work, sacrifice, and commitment to get to where I was personally and professionally. However, without their mentorship and leadership, I would have never been able to leverage my potential.

How did this story make you feel...about you, about me, about my professors and mentors. about my dad, about my life as a young child. about my adult life, about my struggles and triumphs? This is exactly what I love about the power of stories. I share this very story with my students when I want them to feel and to know that sometimes people, even those close to us, underestimate us because of our gender or race or other factors, but if we persevere, we can succeed in spite of their negative opinions. It was difficult for me to share this story. I think I was afraid of being judged for opening the door to my life's story too much. But then, I thought, it would be worse if my life's learnings served no purpose other than my own.

Stories move us and provoke a deeper sense of connection between us and among us. This phenomenon has been happening for thousands of years, well before the advent of the written word. But, why? Why is it that captivating storytelling is distinctly powerful? Neuroscience has provided the validation we needed from science. Using functional magnetic resonance imaging, or fMRI, neuroscientists have been able to track the flow of blood as a mechanism to determine which areas of the brain are active at different times. Incredibly, research using fMRI demonstrates that the activity in listeners' brains synchronizes with the brain activity of the storyteller (Stephens et.al, 2010). In other words, the listeners' and the storyteller's brains are active in the same specific areas while a story is being told with just a short delay in the part of the listener's brain. This may relate to why we find ourselves "captivated" by a story or how storytellers are capable of having audiences "in the palm of their hands."

Stories are one of the most powerful means that we have to actively teach, influence, and even inspire our students. Kendall Haven, award winning author and master storyteller, considers storytelling a foundational ingredient that can be used to influence an individual's current attitude, belief system, knowledge base, and even behavior itself. In his book *Story Proof* (2007), he shares that "results from a dozen prominent cognitive scientists and developmental psychologists have confirmed that human minds *do* rely on stories and story architecture as the primary roadmap for understanding, making sense of, remembering, and planning our lives..."(Haven, 2007). When I think back to my own academic and professional experiences, the most impactful and touching stories are those where the stories were interwoven into the material because they allowed me to experience the world from their perspective, all risk-free. A simple personal story often offered insight into the evolution of their own experience and knowledge which allowed me to see them as more approachable and equally susceptible to the challenges life presents to each of us.

Many professors use true stories to gain the students' attention, to illustrate a complex concept, and to summarize information. Others use fictional stories that closely resemble an authentic true story. Take the example of Dr. Cantor, who provides teaching advice on a website called Course Hero. Dr. Cantor explains on the website that he first got the idea of using storytelling in his teaching while attending a seminar on communication. It helped him realize that stories add emotion and led to student engagement. Therefore, to teach students about the concept of budgeted capacity in managerial accounting—a concept that involves how production departments in a company should be charged back for the use of service department resources—Dr. Cantor walks into the classroom and shares a story about how he just received an invoice from the university's copy center for $250,000 for 150 copies he ordered for his classes. He shares with his students that his department chair is furious with him as the cost for the copies is way too high. How can 150 copies cost so much? He asks students to help him decipher the problem. The point of the story is to teach students how service department costs should be billed to production departments (Course Hero, 2020).

His approach motivates students to learn accounting principles by making the material relatable to them personally through storytelling.

Dr. Cantor also develops a story where his students become supporting protagonists. He begins by asking his students to imagine that they just got a job working for him at a salary of $1,000 a week, receiving paychecks biweekly (every other week). Then, he asks them how much they each have earned after their first week of work. Discussion undoubtedly ensues. "Most say they haven't earned anything," says Dr. Cantor. "But, they have. They just haven't been paid yet." Then he asks them how they would feel if he closed his business down after the first week and refused to pay them. "Well, you owe us the money for one week's pay," they respond. "But," Dr. Cantor responds, "you said you haven't earned anything, right?" Students come to realize that revenue is earned when the services are performed, not when payment is made. He then discusses how his company must show a liability and record a salary expense for the first week's work, even though the salaries have not been paid. Dr. Cantor says, "It focuses the student's mind when they pretend they're talking about their own money and earnings" (Course Hero, 2020).

Dr. Cantor's examples show how stories can be easily interwoven to bring to life a variety of academic areas. I encourage you to think through your life experiences and determine what you can use to help students understand the concept of positive correlations. If there is something in your work or research that moves you, it is all the more likely that it will move your students. Anecdotes, historical narratives, case studies, and allegories are also great places to start.

Below is an example of an analogy I use at the end of a leadership course. Note: I use several candles to help show the students what I mean:

As a new leader, nothing speaks louder to the people you will serve than your generosity. In 1889, Andrew Carnegie wrote an essay titled "Gospel of Wealth." In it, he wisely advises that a wealthy person's life should have two seasons: a time for acquiring wealth and a time for redistributing it. Similarly, I believe a great leader has two lifelong seasons: a time to learn and a time to teach generously. Recently, I read about a popular French author whose work, I believe, exemplifies this very principle. His name is Dominique Lapierre and he traveled to India to conduct research for his new book titled *The City of Joy*. He traveled there on his new Rolls-Royce purchased from a book advance. While there, he found what would change his life forever: what he needed for his book and a passion to help the poor. The back of his business cards read, "All that is not given is lost," by Indian poet Rabindranath Tagore (Lapierre, 1992).

I encourage you to begin giving something that will positively influence the life of others. Do not wait. Generosity should never be an occasional event. It should permeate the life of the effective leader.

How can you cultivate generosity in your life? It is simple. The most valuable thing you can give is your time to someone so that they can become a better version of themselves. You see, the candle I hold in my hand represents me. Many mentors in my life have helped me by providing light to my path (light up the candle). I, in turn, have used my light this semester and, hopefully, I have helped light up your path (I pick up several other candles of different colors and sizes and light each one of them). The beauty of all of this is the fact that your candle loses nothing when it lights another. Quite the contrary...before you know it, there are many, many candles that are now lit because of your generosity. Indeed, your generosity will speak loudly and better serve the people you will be entrusted to lead.

Over the years, I have received emails from graduates referencing this very analogy and sharing their stories of leadership and generosity. This analogy positively inspires students to lead a generous life.

CREATING YOUR OWN STORIES:

This whole concept of the art and science of storytelling was foreign to me. So, I decided to sign up for a couple of Storytelling MasterClasses taught by literary legends, Joyce Carol Oates and Neil Gaiman. While I am still very much a novice, I learned:

1. A great story starts with a great hook intended to immediately catch the attention of your audience. A hook is an interesting incident, question, or problem that encourages the student to keep listening. For example, start your story with an incident, mystery, or problem that the story will eventually solve.

2. Your main character(s) need to be relatable and authentic to your students to the point that your students care about the main character(s). In some cases, if you are scripting a fable or allegory, the characters do not have to be real people or even human. They can be animals or inanimate objects. However, they must feel real in the sense that they are not perfect, but have strengths and weaknesses like everyone else.

3. Develop the central theme, characters, and setting that lead the student down the path toward a resolution. Develop the story from a chronological perspective.

4. Make your ending the ah-ha moment that brings home the central theme of your story. The ending should allude to a truth, moral of the story, resolution, or big meaning.

5. Sometimes, it is possible to share your story without any visuals at all and rely completely on the audience to use their imagination. In other cases, visuals are essential to understand and drive home the message. Visuals can take the form of photographs, drawings, or animations. Visuals, especially animated ones, can help bring the story to life. If you are using images, you do not need to explain each image and, similarly, images can replace words. I suggest listening to how a story is told on NPR or your favorite podcast. A great resource is, *The Moth Podcast.* Pay attention to the tone and pace.

INVITE INTERACTION & ALIGN WITH YOUR LEARNING OBJECTIVES

Just as when you set your learning goals to develop your course, storytelling should start with the end and work backward. While the use of storytelling is compelling, one of the most difficult components of its use in academia is to assess if the story achieved its instructional goals. Therefore, it is important to gather both qualitative and quantitative data to help determine its effectiveness. For example, did the story gain the attention of your students? Did your students enjoy the story? Was it clear to them? Could they recall facts about the story? Did they learn the concept? Could they apply the concept? A technique you can use to assess the value of your stories is the one-minute paper, where I have students write in sixty seconds what they learned in today's lecture. You may also administer a quick quiz assessing for knowledge acquisition or include open-ended questions on your exams. Recently, I had a student answer each open-ended end-of-the-year question by relating her understanding of the content and explaining it via the stories I shared.

Neuroscientific research is validating that storytelling is in fact an effective means of communicating with and holding the attention of others. If you want to be persuasive, storytelling should be in your toolbox.

CHAPTER 5

WHY TEACH AS A HUMAN

"One looks back with appreciation to the brilliant teachers, but with gratitude to those who touched our human feelings."

CARL JUNG

Teaching requires human interaction. Vanessa Rodriguez, Harvard researcher and experienced teacher, compared the teaching process to a chemistry experiment. "You need to understand [the chemicals] independently first in order to understand what's going to happen when you put them together." Conversations about teaching need to recognize that both the teacher and the learner are active participants and work on understanding each participant individually (Rodriguez, 2013).

I believe every instructor has personal stories to tell that connects who they are as people with the content, which in turn can create connections—deep human connections with and for students. For example, I start a lecture on macroaggressions fueled by prejudice as follows, "It took a couple of profound personal experiences for me to genuinely respect the dignity, value, and worth of all people." This is how I start a lecture where we cover the advantages and disadvantages related to mental schemas or assumptions we make about other people. Such a statement leaves students wondering about those personal experiences, so I go on to share detailed information about those experiences that have allowed me to want to be a better human being. Here is what I share:

You see, over the last few years, on the last Friday of November, I've been driving to the local property tax collector's office to pay for real estate taxes. It's honestly not my favorite day of the year; nonetheless, I do it because I know taxes pay for things that I appreciate such as libraries, parks, and emergency services—and also because orange is simply not my color. One year, the dreaded day came. As soon as I finished teaching, I started my annual pilgrimage to the tax collector's office. As I approached the building, I noticed a lady holding a clipboard, speaking to every person as they left the building. I remember thinking, "Oh gosh; I wonder what that's all about. Maybe she is asking for donations and by the time I am done, I will not have much to share." So, I entered the building; I paid my taxes and as I exited, I saw the lady with the clipboard and she saw me too. We exchanged smiles, but that was it. She never approached me.

As I walked away, I heard her talking with the people walking right behind me. So, what do I do?

I walked right back to where she was and I said, "Excuse me ma'am, I noticed you were speaking to every person who exited the building, but you did not speak to me. I just did not want to walk away if there was something I needed to do."

The lady smiled and said, "Oh, I am sorry, I am actually here trying to get people registered to vote and you look like someone who is already registered to vote, so I did not speak to you about it."

"Oh, I see, thank you," I said. I walked away thinking about such an interesting exchange. She thought I was civically responsible simply by the way I was dressed.

A few months later, I happened to be working at one of my newest residential acquisitions. You see, I am also a state certified residential and commercial builder. My husband and I are like Chip and Joanna Gaines of the HGTV show fixer upper, just cuter. We take the ugliest house in a neighborhood and turn it into a dream home. It is something we do for profit of course, but most importantly, because it is our way to contribute to the well-being of our community. So, on this particular day, I was working on the yard. My sweaty hair clung to my face and the knees of my jeans were stained brown from kneeling in the soil. It was definitely not my best look. A little later, I saw a lovely lady with her dog walking toward the house. I stood up, dusted some of the dirt off my hands and walked over to meet her. She asked me if I happened to know if the house was going to be up for sale soon.

I proudly answered: "Oh yes ma'am! I have the open house scheduled for this weekend." The lady went on to say that she had some friends who were interested in buying it. She said she was very pleased as the house made the neighborhood appealing once again and to "please have them put up some information about the open house as we'd love to come by!"

After sharing the above experiences, I engage the students by asking them if they noticed anything about the exchanges

I had with both women. Most of the students immediately respond in disgust: "The second lady kept saying them." "She was so rude and discriminatory." I share that indeed, the second woman had developed a mental schema of what a builder "looked like," and a Hispanic woman working in the garden was not part of that framework. She could not imagine that I was the one who had purchased and restored the house and would be the one selling it. She could not see my worth nor my value as a person beyond the way I looked.

"What did you say to the lady, Dr. Falcon?" is a question that is always asked when I tell this story. I typically and purposefully answer this with a question," I am curious; had you been in a similar situation, what would you have said or done?" Students usually answer something like, "I would have told her I was the builder and she was not invited to the open house" or "I would have cursed at her."

I finish the story with the final punch. I share that I actually felt an overwhelming sense of sadness because of her unwillingness to see the world from a different perspective. Getting mad at her would have been fruitless, as it was really her issue and not mine. You see, I have learned that no matter what she thought of me, it did not change anything about who I am. By responding emotionally, I would have allowed her to gain control of me. Most importantly, I knew to respect her viewpoint even though I wished she would have taken up the opportunity to learn and grow.

I share these two deeply personal experiences to relate and model vulnerability, but it takes a lot of courage to share such experiences with anyone, let alone my students. I learned early, as most of us probably did, that vulnerability indicates weakness, inferiority, and even dependency and, thus, should forever be guarded. However, humanity is waking up to a new understanding from work by thought leader Brené Brown, who argues, "Vulnerability is the core, the heart, and the center of meaningful human experiences" (Brown, 2012).

Perhaps students can use my human stories as a platform on how to live their lives, find their purpose, or just learn how to react to discord and injustice. I share many more stories responsibly that tell about my near misses, my failures, and my successes interwoven as part of a lecture. I believe doing so makes me more authentic and gives the students the freedom to do the same.

If you want to seek deep thinking and authentic responses and processing from students, challenge yourself to tap into your courage and be a bit more human. The payoff is immeasurable.

VULNERABILITY INCREASES CREDIBILITY AND RESPECT

When I was in the corporate world, I quickly learned that you have professional respect, but that does not always yield automatic personal respect. This latter one is built with credibility over time. Professional respect is what is owed to a teacher, police officer, physician, and others who have positions of authority. This kind of respect is not personally earned, but is expected because of the official position or job the person has. However, it has nothing to do with how you feel or think about the person, it is about honoring their position of authority. Such respect is shown by being polite.

Personal respect, on the other hand, is earned by being trustworthy and empathetic. As professors, we excel by being competent, but also for being kind and displaying other positive personal characteristics. I believe that when you respect people, with both professional and personal respect as appropriate, and if you always make sure your conduct and dealings with people are honorable, trustworthy, competent, and kind, you will have genuinely earned the respect of others. I have learned over time that if we share the ups *and* downs and the struggles of our human experience in the right way in the right context, we build deeper connections.

I actually learned this valuable lesson unexpectedly. I had just completed a review of several medical charts because a whistleblower reported unethical documentation practices by one of my most capable and loved supervisors. I started the review thinking that perhaps it was an error of perception. This particular supervisor had been doing this type of work for over ten years; she was a mentor to many and a great leader. As I reviewed the charts, I noted a pattern that was not supposed to be there. Astonished, I added more records to the initial sample size. Indeed, I had corroborated what I simply did not want to believe to be true. I actually took the afternoon off just to reflect on my next steps. My experience told me that I had to fire the supervisor, as the facts in front of me portrayed person with lack of judgement. I wrestled with giving her an opportunity and not terminating her employment. However, I knew it was going to be very difficult for me to trust her even if she no longer was a supervisor.

The next day, I met with her. I had one last hope that she had a reasonable explanation. She did not. In fact, she shared that she had been waiting for this moment to come, as she knew her behavior was wrong but her desire to please everyone had gotten the best of her. We both cried as she said, "Where do you need me to sign?" I handed her the termination letter and she signed it and left the room. I was just devastated. I then gathered myself as best I could and went on to speak to her staff members. For privacy reasons, I could not share with them the reasons behind the termination but had to tell them that for now, they all reported to me until a new supervisor was assigned. The staff members were visibly upset. As I prepared to leave the room, they all started to walk toward me and hugged me. The tears I had hidden had nowhere else to go but out. It was the first time in over fifteen years of being a successful leader that I ever cried in front of my staff.

My first mentor and supervisor taught me to never share my emotions with staff for I would be viewed as a weak and insecure leader. That is what my mind was telling me to do, but my heart and soul had other plans. After the group hug, no more words were exchanged. I was emotionally drained. I went to my office, picked up my keys, and left for the refuge of home. I was in pain and had let my mentor down. A few hours later, Sandy, one of the staff members, called me on her way home. She said, "Today was a hard day, but I want you to know we all respect you very much because we know you care for each of us as persons. We know that because we saw you hurting today." My vulnerability had allowed me to break down the role I played as a boss and connect with the others as humans. This experience changed me as a leader and as a person for the better.

As I transitioned to academia, I noticed some professors acting as if they were owed respect given their title, experience, and/or research output. Perhaps this is true to a certain extent. However, if there is anything I learned from the corporate world, it's that you cannot demand respect and expect to receive it. You have to earn it. How? You do so by first lowering our defenses and dropping the idea that we are a superior being compared to our students. At the end of the day, we are the same—we just have the advantage of having had accumulated more wisdom. As such, I think we are the first ones to recognize that we do not have all of the answers. In doing so, we show that we are vulnerable, fallible humans too. It is scary to step into the unknown and let down your guard with students, but there is no other way to earn the respect that will let us grow into the professor/leader we aim to be.

VULNERABILITY WITH COLLEAGUES

Vulnerability is also valuable when speaking with colleagues. During our professional development sessions at the start of each semester, we all learn from one another and feel free to share what we struggle with, where we have found treasure, and most importantly, how we can help each other in order to become more engaging teachers for our students. I believe this is only possible because our leadership does a lot of work to cultivate trust and a strong desire to see us be successful in the classroom. If any one of us is feeling that something is not going well in the classroom, I know there are a host of faculty members who are willing to help me think things through objectively.

That is one of the most awesome things about our school. Our professional community allows us—even when the work is challenging—to feel that we are not alone in the work. We all know we learn better together and that our work benefits from the perspective of others. For example, as faculty, we have a Facebook page exclusively to help each other over the course of the semester. I believe one of the most remarkable traits of all great leaders is their relentless pursuit of wisdom and understanding. As faculty and scholars, we find ourselves in the constant cycle of knowledge, comprehension, questioning, discovery, and application that goes on our entire lives. Now, that is vulnerability.

TEACHING WITH HUMANITY:

Not even a year into my new career as an academic, I had an experienced that showed me the importance of being empathetic to my students. I was teaching a personal finance course and I had developed a simple assignment where students were to imagine their future professional selves. They were to take their current resumé, select a job description of the position they aimed to secure in the future, and essentially conduct a resumé gap analysis to identify what they needed to work on to add to their resumé. They were to submit a thoughtful assessment and outline a few short, intermediate, and long-term plans to achieve their desired job. I was very proud of this assignment, for my goal was to not only have them create a workable plan to achieve a future goal, but also to give them hope and a glimpse into their future should they work hard and follow a strategy. All but one student turned in the assignment on time. Since I do not accept late work, I proceeded to grade the assignments and just gave an F to the student who did not complete it.

A couple of weeks went by and I began to notice that he did not submit any other subsequent assignments. One day, after class, I made it a point to speak with him about his declining grade. He shared with me that he was having some personal problems, but he would work to ensure all future assignments were completed. His explanation and commitment to change his recent pattern diminished my concern. As the semester went on, his inconsistency in turning in assignments continued. I approached him after class again and asked him to stop by my office during my office hours. He did the next day. We talked about the assignments coming up and provided additional guidance by going over the instructions and reviewing some content. As expected, he submitted his assignments on time. Toward the end of the semester, he stopped by my office and said, "Dr. Falcon, I just want to apologize for not completing the resumé gap analysis assignment," to which I responded, "Well, I do wish you would have spent time completing it because it was intended to give you a glimpse into your future self."

He then opened his notebook and showed me his work on this assignment. It was several pages of unfinished written notes. He proceeded to tell me that he suffered from depression and anxiety and that his medication had been changed just prior to coming to college. He shared he had been struggling and had been receiving services from our counseling center. He explained that, at the time the assignment was due, he just could not even contemplate his future. He went on to explain that he grabbed on to the assignment with all of his might and worked on it each day until he could finally see his future self. He went on to thank me for a great semester and for spending extra time going over assignments during my office hours. After he left my office, I realized my goal for the assignment had been met and having seen his work, I broke my own rule for no late assignments and gave him a few points for having attempted it. While it did not change his overall grade, I knew he would see that I honored his effort. I learned, as Dr. Brené Brown would put it, "to feel with people" (Brown, 2016).

Having not been a student for many years, it is difficult for many of us to empathize. So how do we become better at it? At the beginning of this year, a *Wall Street Journal* article grabbed me from its title, "How to Teach Professors Humility?

Hand Them a Rubik's Cube," authored by Melissa Korn (Korn, 2021). In essence, the article conveys the experience of a few professors from a couple of universities who were challenged to learn how to solve a Rubik's Cube. For those professors who already had mastered the task, they were given a more complex Rubik's Cube. All professors were given a few weeks to learn how to do it. They were also given educational videos showing them how to solve the cubes, written step-by-step directions, and scholarly articles about the benefits of learning how to solve the cube through an online platform.

They were to click submit when they achieved solving it successfully in five minutes or less. One-third of the participants did not complete the assignment on time as the frenetic pace of the semester picked up. The ones who did achieve the goal developed their own strategies, among which included creating a study group and not even watching the videos. Why did they do this with their faculty? They wanted faculty to be able to empathize with students learning something really challenging and new that they never learned before. Based on the narrative contained in the article about the professor's struggles with the assignment, you can see the faculty did come away from the experience recognizing that they had forgotten what it is like to be a novice—what it is like to be in the students' shoes.

What is important in this conversation is to begin designing your teaching plan from their novice perspective. Teddy Roosevelt once said, "Nobody cares how much you know until they know how much you care" (Lam, 2019). If you show you care, your students will learn more and without a doubt, you will earn their respect.

CHAPTER 6

WHAT NEEDS TO CHANGE

"If you don't like something, change it. If you can't change it, change your attitude."

MAYA ANGELOU

Imagine a man is in his kitchen helping his daughter with her history homework. She is looking for answers about the time when Mount Vesuvius erupted. He looks to Alexa for answers about the destroyed city without his daughter noticing and simply relays to his daughter the information he receives from the voice assistant. This scenario was the basis of a recent Amazon Echo commercial where the tag line was "a voice is all you need" (Amazon Alexa: Pompeii, 2021).

Indeed, a voice command is all you need to leverage information in seconds on any subject known to man. So why is our education system so focused on relaying information? I believe education must move from a framework of disseminating information to one where students can understand the logical connection between ideas. We need discussion, exploration, and testing in the field. We need enhanced experiences with other humans. We need to front-load the philosophy, process through experience, and then regroup and reorient. These are things Alexa and Amazon Echo cannot do (at least yet) for us all.

We need to help develop the next generation of citizens who can, at the very least, determine the importance and relevance of arguments and ideas, identify inconsistencies and errors in reasoning, and reflect on the justification of their own assumptions, beliefs, and values. In short, we as higher education professors need to develop critical thinkers. I recently had the opportunity to speak with a couple of hiring managers who shared with me that they are keenly and sadly aware of the huge gap between what students learn during their post-secondary education and what they need for them to do on the job. Their assessment was corroborated by a 2018 Bloomberg Next and Workday survey, which reported only 35 percent of employers across the nation report feeling confident that new recruits are well prepared with hard technical skills and soft skills such as, agility and adaptability, team working skills, complex problem solving, ethical judgement, and analytical reasoning. To make matters worse, the report identified that business and academia are not closely collaborating to reduce this widening gap. In fact, only 30 percent of corporations and 39 percent of educators reported to be actively collaborating to help reskill and retrain employees.

So why are recruiters still hiring these candidates? Partly because we have experienced a historically low unemployment rate so they have to hire to remain competitive. They reduce the knowledge gap by having corporate training programs focused on closing the gap efficiently so that their new employee can add value as quickly as possible.

In addition to the required hard skills or knowledge base, recruiters and employers are unlikely to be impressed by candidates unless they can demonstrate a certain degree of people skills. As the impact of AI and disruptive technology grows, candidates who can perform tasks that machines cannot rise to the top as they add value to the corporations on day one. In a 2017 Manpower Group survey of two thousand employers, over 50 percent of organizations listed problem solving, collaboration, customer service, and communication as the most valued skills (Talent Shortage Survey, 2018). Likewise, a recent report by Josh Bersin, global industry analyst, noted that employers today are as likely to select candidates for their adaptability, culture fit, and growth potential as for in-demand technical skills (e.g., python, analytics, cloud computing) (Bersin, 2020). Employers like Microsoft, Amazon, and Google have highlighted the importance of learnability, which is defined as the ability to be curious and have an inquisitive mind as key indicators of career potential—both of which, by the way, are also not cultivated via an educational system dependent on lectures and passive learners.

IS MORE ALWAYS BETTER?

Before the 2020 pandemic, we had a growing number of people graduating with a bachelor's degree. According to the 2019 College Board Education Pays Report, the percentage of eighteen- to twenty-four-year-olds who enrolled in college increased to 41 percent in 2018 from 25 percent in 1978. This enrollment growth translates into 67 percent of adults aged twenty-five to thirty-four have at least some level of college experience in 2018 marking a 20 point increase since 1980. (College Board, 2019). This statistic is positive from the perspective of higher salaries. In 2020, the U.S. Bureau of

Labor Statistics released a report that found a positive correlation between a higher worker's educational attainment and increased earnings. Additionally, the higher a person's educational level, the less likely they were to be unemployed. In terms of overall lifetime earnings, the average worker with a bachelor's degree may earn approximately $1 million more than a worker without a postsecondary education.

Moreover, increase in wages generates higher tax payments at local, state, and federal levels supporting social support programs such as unemployment compensation, Social Security, Medicare, and the Supplemental Nutrition Assistance Program (SNAP). Individuals with a high school diploma are four times more likely to access SNAP benefits than those with a bachelor's degree or higher. What's more, the benefits of college education, according to the College Board's report, extend well beyond higher salaries. More educated citizens have greater access to healthcare and retirement plans, exercise more, spend more time reading to their children, volunteer, vote, and can provide better opportunities for their children.

The upward trend in college enrollment was ravaged by the 2020 COVID-19 pandemic, as tertiary education, similar to all other industries, was also not immune to its devastating effects. According to the National Student Clearinghouse Research Center, roughly one month into the fall 2020 semester, undergraduate enrollment was running 4 percent below 2018 levels. Higher education lost about four hundred thousand students in the fall of 2020. Doug Shapiro, executive director of the National Student Clearinghouse Research Center, shared that entering freshman students had the largest decline of any group with a decrease of 16.1 percent at the national level. Perhaps more concerning is the reported 22.7 percent drop of freshman students attending community colleges. The decline equates to more than six hundred thousand students not enrolling at community colleges, according to Walter G. Bumphus, president and CEO of the American Association of Community Colleges.

To make matters worse, two important shifts were noted by Todd Sedmak: 1) the pattern of increased college enrollment during economic downturns was disrupted, especially for two- and four-year community colleges, which historically experience larger increases in enrollment during economic recessions, and 2) the largest enrollment declines in the four-year college sector were among students with the strongest academic credentials (e.g., high school GPAs of A and A+), who were replaced by similar increases in the enrollment rates of students with weaker academic credentials (e.g., B- and lower students) (Sedmak, 2020).

But let's not despair just yet. According to a *Wall Street Journal* article published in March of 2021 titled, "College Admission Season is Crazier than Ever," our nation's "most-selective four-year colleges and universities" saw a record-breaking 17 percent increase in applications this year, according to the Common Application. For an enrollment driven industry, this is great news. However, regardless of how the college enrollment numbers change over the post pandemic era, producing graduates without the skills needed speaks poorly about our education system and our ability as professors to adapt our teaching to meet what the work force demands. A recent report by Burning Glass (2018) suggests that 20 percent of graduates are not working at a job that requires a college education even ten years post-graduation. In addition, to make matters worse, the report adds, technology is changing at such rapid speed that "future jobs will be hard to predict, except for the fact that they will require a very different range of skills than that displayed by most graduates. That's why the future potential of the workforce will depend on its ability to cultivate learnability, rather than displaying lots of college credentials."

SEIZING THE OPPORTUNITY

From a historical perspective, it is clear that the benefits and opportunities a higher education provides far outweigh the decision not to pursue a higher education degree. The unprecedented challenges brought about by the pandemic provide a pivotal opportunity for higher education administrators and professors to rethink and reevaluate each key infrastructure component such as tuition fees, course delivery, course offerings, student support, teacher development offerings, academic calendars, and fundraising. Returning to the enduring sameness is as unthinkable as the disruptions caused by COVID-19. It is a great moment to think about and highlight the things no one else can do as well as universities and focus on restoring their relevance by helping narrow the gap and produce graduates who have the knowledge and skills necessary to navigate our unpredictable world. In doing so, colleges and universities have the unique opportunity to substantially increase the value of the college degree by aligning curriculum with demand, providing the platform to allow professors more flexibility to teach students the hard skills as well as spend more time teaching students critical soft skills.

If colleges and universities simply go back to the pre-pandemic educational model, there could be a significant risk by having industry disruptors redefine the industry. However, at least as of now, no clear alternative to universities has yet emerged despite the existential threat placed by disruptors such as massive open online courses (MOOCs) such as Udacity and Coursera. The logic of why MOOCs presented such a threat to the existing higher educational model ten years ago was reasonably sound. Faced with an option of quality courses that were free, why would people continue to go into debt to take courses from universities and colleges? Well, it is simple: it turned out that free is not a crowd-drawing factor after all. The dropout rate of MOOCs was amazingly high.

In an article published by *Science* in January of 2019, Justin Reich and co-author Jose Ruperez-Valiente explain that when retention in MOOCs is measured, on average, only 55 percent of people who enrolled actually watch the first video. Actually, the major issue with why universities have not been affected by MOOCs is to do with a range of factors that are integral to the way universities work. Universities are governed by legislation and quality requirements that restrict who can award a degree and how they have to go about ensuring that students achieve a particular standard in order to earn that degree. This has made any change to this model a matter for governments as well as universities and their customers. Thus, at least for now, allowing credits for individual MOOCs to count toward a degree has not gained much traction.

However, there are pain points that those of us in the education field and beyond could be confronting. For example, some companies had already begun the task reframing educational models in order to remain competitive:

- Google is partnering with community colleges, opening a new pathway offering students an IT Support Professional Certificate. The courses are offered through Coursera or at the community college as part of either a set of non-credit courses or as a full credit set courses required to earn an associate degree (Zinshteyn, 2020).

- In 2018, Northern Virginia Community College partnered with Amazon to offer cloud computing. Scott Ralls, the college's president, noted that it was a necessary move to match the supply of qualified candidates to the region's highest IT job demands in the nation (NOVA, 2018).
- General Assembly, a coding boot camp, reported website traffic increasing from 175,111 visitors in April 2019 to 314,559 visitors in April 2020—an increase of 179 percent (McKenzie, 2020).
- The City University of Seattle is collaborating with Amazon Global Military Affairs Program and now offers various focused skill certificates designed for working adults and former members of the military (Romano, 2020).
- The Gies College of Business partnered with Coursera and is offering an MBA program for less than $25,000. The move caused a 35 percent increase in the number of applicants from August 2019 to August 2020 (Byrne, 2020).

These initiatives, if nothing else, should provide a foundation to inform much of the work higher education needs to do to reimagine its future.

SO, HOW CAN WE CONTINUE TO MAKE COLLEGE EDUCATION RELEVANT IN THESE CHANGING TIMES?

STOP OVERPROMISING AND UNDER DELIVERING

I have spent time reviewing hundreds of college and university admissions websites, as I was curious about how or what they offer as their value preposition to potential new students. In doing so, I noticed that admissions typically market heavily highlighting graduating senior's levels of employability and success. I believe these marketing tactics produce very high expectations that are not feasible to fulfill at scale. As my colleague, Celina Jozsi would say, "Not everyone can be a leader, a CEO, or a highly sought-after consultant." It is just not possible to give everyone their dream job. If our students' career aspirations surpass the available job opportunities and their self-perceived talents exceed their actual talents, they are surely destined to be miserable at work. I understand the need to speak to the successes; however, I believe it is more important to advertise faculty-to-student ratios for freshman courses, four-year student graduation rates, opportunities for service learning, and finally, yet importantly, who is responsible for academic advising. This last topic is of extreme importance and perhaps where the real value preposition is found.

Academic advising is one of the two most important levers to pull within the university to positively impact student success (the other, creating a learning-centered curriculum in the classroom) that should be promoted, and quite frankly, explained as a must have to prospective students and their parents. It is academic advising that "provides perhaps the only opportunity for all students to develop a personal, consistent relationship with someone in the institution who cares about them," according to Jane Drake in her 2016 article on student persistence (Drake, 2016). As an academic advisor, I can attest to that and it is not only consistency and caring that are important—I am able to facilitate a student's level of self-awareness leading to the discovery of unique talents and encouraging degree completion.

HIRE EFFECTIVE TEACHERS

Despite much evidence to the contrary, I have realized that there is a common belief in academia that being an expert in a discipline makes you an effective teacher of it. I think the "everyone can teach" idea makes teaching appear less technical than it actually is. According to a white paper published in 2017 by the Association of College and University Educators (ACUE), "many part-time professors, who now make up a majority share of the nation's faculty workforce, still rely heavily on traditional lecture based teaching practices that contradict the latest findings on how people learn. It's not only the part-timers of whom this is true, but an overwhelming majority of these adjuncts receive no resources for professional development." Forty years of educational research consistently yields that instructors are a key variable affecting student outcomes (Gordon, 2012). A growing body of literature indicates that effective teaching improves students' critical thinking and persistence and "when faculty improve their teaching, students learn more, and their performance on course work improves" (Condon, Iverson, Manduca, Rutz, and Willett, 2016). So why not start hiring and keeping only effective professors who are also experts in their discipline?

IT'S TIME TO CHANGE WHAT WE VALUE

Most universities require their professors to show a high level of proficiency in teaching, research, and service to the college and/or community. Theoretically, all three components are weighted into three equal parts however, the professional university ladder requires the publishing of research to achieve higher levels. In fact, if we go under the assumption that we put our money where it matters, a recent finding by

Paul Courant and Sarah Turner found that faculty salaries at research universities are determined primarily by two factors: their research performance and the reputation that comes along with it.

As a relative newcomer into the industry, I do not understand this idea that we can do all three functions exceptionally. If our primary and most important function in higher education is to teach, motivate, and develop lifelong learners, why not reward exceptional teaching as much as the creation of new knowledge (research) during our annual performance evaluation? Or, better yet, we should capitalize on each professor's strengths and individual aptitude. In other words, let exceptional teachers teach and let exceptional researchers research and coach everyone in the center either toward exceptionalism or out the door. This is exactly what high performing businesses do.

That is not to say that there are professors who can't be both exceptional teachers and exceptional researchers. In fact, a study by two Northwestern University professors suggests that tenured faculty can be both effective teachers and skilled scholars at the same time. In other words, skilled scholars do not come at the expense of exceptional pedagogy, or vice versa. In it, Schapiro and his co-author David Figlio measured data from all first-year undergraduates students at the university between 2001 and 2008. They measured teaching quality of tenured faculty two ways.

First, they measured the rate at which non-majors became majors. For example, if a student with an undeclared major took a biology class and subsequently became a biology major, that student's professor would be marked as inspirational.

Second, they measured "deep learning" by how well students performed in more advanced classes in the same field. The authors measured research excellence of tenured faculty through two indicators as well. First, they counted university recognition and second, they computed each faculty member's "h-index," which measures frequency and influence of research publications. Interestingly, at Northwestern at least, these indicators had no relationship, suggesting that some faculty can be both ineffective teachers and poor researchers—or one or the other as well.

It's unclear how much this study of Northwestern students and faculty can apply to other colleges around the country, but certainly Schapiro and Figlio provide an excellent model for colleges and universities to compute the data for their own institutions and find out how they compare. Additionally, their study focused on tenured faculty who, by the mere fact they have been tenured, possess a higher level of expertise both in teaching and research because they have much more experience than a junior faculty member and certainty more than an adjunct professor.

ALLOW TIME TO WORK ON PEDAGOGY

In 2014, anthropologist John Ziker, from Boise State University (BSU), published an unprecedented study on how university professors spend their time. Frankly, I am quite astonished that a time study such as this one had not been conducted before as in industry, as we are all about finding ways to reduce time inefficiencies, which can bankrupt any business. Dr. Ziker's report, named "TAWKS" (Time Allocation Workload Knowledge Study), set out to quantify the faculty work patterns and productivity (Ziker et. al., 2014).

Dr. Ziker's results showed just how our work as professors is riddled with inefficiencies. Using a modified version of the anthropological technique "24-hour recall," thirty tenure-track and tenured professors from BSU were asked to report everything they did from 4 a.m. on the previous day to the day of the recall interview. On average, Dr. Ziker found that the study participants worked sixty-one hours per week and just under ten hours over the weekend. Combining workweek and weekend, Dr. Ziker found that faculty spent approximately 40 percent of their time on teaching-related activities, or about 24.5 hours, which is 60 percent of a forty-hour week to put it in perspective (Ziker et al., 2014).

His findings from nearly ten years ago still ring somewhat true, at least based on the many conversations I have had with colleagues. Just taking a small sample size of ten of my colleagues from various departments, we are all working on average, fifty-five hours during the week and approximately ten hours on the weekend. The lion share of our time is spent in grading papers, making copies, writing letters of recommendations, attending meetings, responding to emails, writing letters of recommendation, (No, that is not a typo, it seems like a never-ending task), re-teaching material during office hours, advancing our research—oh, and yes, preparing for the next class. There is often little to no time to reflect on pedagogy and educational activities to enhance our teaching (Ziker et al., 2014).

Perhaps we need to conduct more time studies to truly understand faculty workload at each university setting so that more informed decisions could be made about where and how we are spending our time and we can reduce non-value-added activities.

KEEP ENCOURAGING INNOVATION

There is much we all have gained from pivoting during the current pandemic. With faculty and students alike forced to rethink how education is delivered, I have been witness to some of the most dramatic advancements in educational pedagogy ever. Examples of new teaching innovation are everywhere. Most professors have been able to successfully integrate students and alumni in the classroom seamlessly online without great coordination of schedules, physical travel, etc. Additionally, faculty have invited multiple alumni to join classes further enriching integrated class discussions.

I have also witnessed faculty using free group messaging apps such as GroupMe as a pedagogical tool to facilitate online course discussions, small group work, and other course communications both in face-to-face and online sections. Research by Susie Gronseth and Waneta Herbert. from the University of Houston, supports the use instant messaging platforms such as GroupMe, as their findings indicated it "afforded students opportunities to engage in productive course-relevant conversations and provided additional ways for learners to exhibit online social presence through tool features."

I also noticed professors moving more toward capturing their lectures through easy-to-use software. such as Screencastify, and then using their class time (either online or in person) to effectively help students practice the material, give them time to ask questions, and provide a deeper view into the why now that the how is out of the way.

EMPHASIZE SERVICE LEARNING

Almost thirty years ago, Ernest Boyer wrote an excellent article in *The Chronicle of Higher Education* where he makes the point that for over one hundred years (from the 1860s to 1960s), our nation's universities have included service as a mission. "But what about today?" he asked. "I am concerned that in recent years, higher education's historic commitment to service seems to have diminished. I am troubled that many now view the campus as a place where professors get tenured and students get credentialed" (Boyer, 1994).

Boyer called for a "New American College," one that "celebrates teaching and selectively supports research, while also taking special pride in its capacity to connect thought to action, theory to practice." Boyer argued, "students urgently need to connect what they learn with how they live."

His words certainty resonated with me and I am sure they do for you as well. Having been afforded the opportunity to lead service learning at our school, I have been able to experience that service learning allows students to learn about their capacity to serve others, increase empathy, understand the meaning of responsible citizenship, grow in the awareness of cultural differences, and refine their decision making and leadership abilities. Wow. Now that is a list of learning objectives!

From a programmatic perspective, our colleges and universities support and promote extracurricular community partnerships extraordinarily well. Students actively participate through student organizations, student life, and campus-based religious organizations. I believe service learning has been integrated into the fabric of most of our nation's colleges and institutions. However, to truly evolve our commitment, I believe service learning needs to be a credit-bearing educational experience in which students participate in an organized service activity that meets identified community needs. They should reflect on the service activity as a way to gain further understanding of course content, a broader appreciation of the discipline, and an enhanced sense of civic responsibility.

One great example of what is possible to do is an organization called Enactus. It was originally founded in the US in 1975 and now it has expanded into thirty-six countries around the world. Out of the over roughly four thousand universities in the US, only 317 universities, amounting to fewer than six thousand students, participate. The vision of Enactus is to engage students in entrepreneurial action to improve the world (Enactus.org).

Students plan and implement novel and innovative solutions to address a problem they identify within their community, state, or even in another nation. Students are provided an opportunity to showcase their work and accomplishments at the annual US National Competition, where their innovative ideas are judged by a panel of corporate business leaders who assess how their work improved the quality of life and standard of living of those in need. The winner of the competition moves on to compete at the Enactus World Cup. Enactus has provided a window into a remarkable, ongoing engagement forum for our students. I have witnessed students being remarkable agents of constructive change. Enactus is a perfect example that movement in this direction is possible if we as faculty are willing to accept service learning as a legitimate curricular tool.

CHAPTER 7

HOW TO INCORPORATE GAME-BASED LEARNING

"You will either step forward into growth or you will step back into safety."

ABRAHAM MASLOW

"Is class already over?"

This is my favorite question from a student after we have played an educational game or simulation.

Losing track of time after engaging in the learning process is one attribute of cognitive engagement that closely resembles critical thinking. Some other attributes of cognitive engagement include persevering, learning from experiences, and sharing the learning and collaborating with others (Fisher et al., 2017).

I first learned about educational games by attending professional training corporate programs. They aim to capture and retain the learner's attention, engage them through meaningful narrative, challenge them, provide feedback, and provide a sense of accomplishment and recognition. From this prior experience, I wondered if I could use some of those games in the classroom to provide context or introduce a concept. To answer the question, I researched and found overwhelming evidence that effective pedagogy involves students interacting with one another, solving problems, analyzing issues, creating a business, debating ideas or different points of view, evaluating evidence, or generating hypotheses. In short, the evidence points to active learning as a way to enhance critical thinking and the application of the concepts beyond the classroom (Bonwell & Eison, 1991; Prince, 2004; Bachman and Bachman, 2011).

Machemer and Crawford did not negate the need for lectures, but added that active learning activities as a way to augment lectures, "provides opportunities for students to reflect, evaluate, analyze, synthesize, and communicate on or about the information being presented" (Machemer and Crawford, 2017). As I began to implement active learning to complement my lectures, I began to see students reacting to the lectures with comments and additional questions, participating in class discussions, and ultimately becoming involved in their learning. In his 2016 book, *Excellent Sheep*, William Deresiewicz (2016) eloquently explained,

> "I myself became a decent teacher only when I started to relinquish some control over the classroom - stopped worrying so much about 'getting my points across' and recognized that those moments of disorder that would sometimes occur, those spontaneous outbreaks of intelligence, were the most interesting parts of the class, for both the students and me. We were going somewhere new, and we were going there together."

The focus had changed. At last, active learning had emerged triumphantly as the catalyst for inquiry, curiosity, engagement, and innovation. It was all I needed to fuel the courage to try to break the traditional lecture mold. The more I worked to incorporate and perfect more activities into my lectures, the more I noticed student interest in my courses. In fact, many students began to email me requesting an additional seat in my class, often citing the interactive learning as a key component drawing them into my class.

During that same time, I also began inquiring how to create a sense of belonging within the classroom. I desired to create a part of a "we" culture, and yet provide a space for each student to feel moved to speak their own individuality. In doing so, I turned to Priya Parker's book, *The Art of Gathering.* I learned that any gathering, including a classroom, needs a purpose. Without one, the gathering centers solely on the mechanics of stuff like PowerPoints, AV equipment, and handouts. So part of the idea of creating that human connection starts and ends with a purpose to make the environment one in which students feel empowered to speak, participate, engage in activities, and learn (Parker, 2020).

I turned to books to find out how to create such an environment and how to best implement game-based learning. Finding little guidance, I focused on developing my own approach. Many professors I have talked to want to incorporate more of these techniques, but are not sure where to start. Here are ten tips I have found helpful to foster a more engaged classroom environment:

1. The First Day of Class

As the saying goes, you never get a second chance to make a first impression. So, resist the urge to go over the syllabus. On the first day of class, I spend about five to ten minutes sharing my passion for the subject matter, why I believe the course will be of value to their professional lives, what I expect of them as students, and what they can expect of me in return. In other words, I focus on setting clear ground rules and connecting them to a common purpose of learning.

In order to cover other important information contained on the syllabus, I rely on a short assessment in the form of a quiz due ahead of the first day of class. I find this practice to be an excellent preamble to my expectation of students being prepared for class. Additionally, it allows me to spend most of our first class session getting to know the students instead of the students getting to know the syllabus.

I typically play the game "Whodunit" or "I'm an Acronym" (you can find these in the games section of this book) as community building or warm-up activities, which engage the students and bring a sense of fun and positivity to the classroom environment. Through this exercise, I am able to quickly learn the students' names on the first day of class, as I am able to connect their name to a fact they have shared about themselves as part of the warm up activity.

I rely heavily on index cards for these activities. I ask students to write their name on the back as well as their favorite song. I have students leave their index card at their desk for me to retrieve at the end of the first class. As I collect the index cards, I complete a seating chart, which allows me to take attendance and also provides me with a secondary method to help me memorize all of my students' name by the second day of class.

My experience using these warm-up activities has been extraordinary. Every start of the semester, students stay after class just to say they are looking forward to the class and my teaching methodology. I remember one day I had just finished the first day of class and, as I walked toward my office, the janitor stopped me and said, "Your students are coming out of your classroom happy and talking to one another...I have never seen that before...that's amazing!" Indeed, it is an amazing feeling to start the semester with such synergy.

2. Make the Classroom a Joyful Place For Learning

Music can make us feel different emotions. I come in early to class and play songs from the repertoire of my students' favorite songs shared on the first day of class. Sometimes, I use some of my favorite songs from Jack Johnson or other upbeat instrumental music. When I play my own selection of top soft rock music from the '80s and '90s, students tend to engage in conversation inquiring about the music, adding an additional layer of personal connection. Be mindful of the volume. I typically just play it as background music that is noticeable but does not hinder conversation among students. Yes, that last point is worth repeating. When you create a community of learners, they actually walk into the classroom greeting one another and engaging in conversation instead of just looking at their phones. They stop being islands and become a community.

Additionally, I have found music energizes students while they are working on an educational activity. I usually play music based on the game. For example, if it is a problem solving activity, I play Jeopardy's theme song, jazz, or classical music. If it is an activity where students are conducting an activity such as building a spaghetti tower, I play the top twenty clean version songs of the year.

3. Use an Agenda Each Class Session

At the onset of each class session, I share with students what the purpose or goal is for the lecture, share the name and objective of the learning activity we will participate in, and remind them of any future assignments and due dates. I have found it is important for students to know what we will be discussing and why early on. Students learn to look forward to the educational game and pay more attention to the lecture because they learn they will have to apply the concepts learned.

I have also learned that the anticipation of a game brings joy to the classroom. In this moment of multiple elongated crises, I believe that we need all the joy we can get.

4. Start Each Class Session by Asking Students to Share What They Have Learned So Far

The first item on the agenda is to do a "check-in." Here is where I invite students to share one thing they have learned this semester as a way to reorient them to the class content learned thus far. After a couple of minutes of discussion, we arrive to the topic of the last class session, which allows me to use it as a platform upon which to build the next content. It also provides me with a quick assessment of whether the objectives for the last class session were met or if I need to reinforce any of the previous content before I move on.

It is important to note that at first, some students do not know really what to do or how to behave, for all students seem to be preconditioned to be passive receivers of information. However, this practice, coupled with the educational games, has allowed me to create an educational environment where students see themselves as contributors of insights and fresh ideas. I believe all students, not just the ones who are good at memorizing information, begin to see themselves as good students who can think critically and become inspired to learn.

5. Ask Open-Ended Questions during the Part of the Class Where Content Is Introduced via Lecture

I call upon individual students by name to answer questions to keep the class attentive. I usually ask a question where I invite them to compare, contrast, and share their reaction to the content every three to four minutes so that students are constantly on their toes. While it is great to call upon the students who raise their hands, I usually call upon a student who did not and invite them to share. Yes, cold calling is important. In order to create psychological safety where students feel comfortable speaking up asking a question, taking an interpersonal risk and even offering an idea that they are not sure it is a good answer, I turn to their classmate community. I usually say something like, "Okay, tell me more," as a way to have the student offer more detail to their thought process, and then I invite other students to join the discussion so that all students are listening and feeling compelled to speak and rescue one another.

By the second or third week of classes, students seem to adapt and are typically ready for me when I call upon them to answer. I have found this particular approach very useful, especially for introverted students who experience difficulty speaking in front of others. It also reinforces the need for students to be prepared before class.

I recently had an opportunity to attend an online seminar held by Bryan University professor Dr. Mike Roberto, who spoke about his experience cold calling students. He, as many of us do, provides a grade to students for their thoughtful contributions in class. Each class session, he selects three students and hands them a document containing the class roster. He instructs the three students to identify the top three contributors to that class session's collective learning. He points out that their job is not to track how many times someone speaks, but rather the richness of their discussion contributions. They are to write only positive comments by the student's name and each of them is to select the top three contributors and turn it in to him. By the end of the semester, Dr. Roberto has a rich body of evidence that allows for grading student participation. He also believes this practice positively contributes to the creation of psychological safety in the classroom, as there is no negative element. Students are only rewarded for contributing to the learning.

6. Incorporate Videos, Documentaries, Parts of TED Talks into the Lecture

Incorporating a video or TED Talk allows us to show more and tell less when introducing students to new information, concepts, and skills. They help amplify the curriculum as it is another way to make key information comprehensible. It is important to pick the most dynamic and telling parts of the film, news segment, or documentary to show students. However, first and foremost, be clear on your purpose—that will help you determine what to show and how to frame it for students.

It is equally important that before you show the video, you provide students with a purpose before playing the video. For example, "As you watch, I want you to pay close attention to..." Setting a goal for what students are about to watch will keep them accountable and attentive.

I give students time to reflect by pausing the video. I try to avoid having students write notes or answering questions while they watch. Pausing every few minutes allows the students time to process what they're viewing. I also tend to use the scaffolding pedagogy strategy by using the same clips at different times of the semester so that students can begin to experience how their newly acquired knowledge is allowing them to appreciate and analyze the same information at a deeper level.

7. Start With Games/Activities That Are Engaging and Short at First

Keep in mind that high-energy activities can intimidate students, especially those whose natures are more reserved or quiet. Remember, the goal is to get them in the habit of engaging so that by the end of the semester, they are more than willing to participate in higher-energy activities. With this in mind, I begin by incorporating shorter activities at the onset of the semester. Students begin to get used to these activities as the semester goes on.

Keep in mind that these games or activities can be incorporated before you introduce the concept via lecture, in the middle of a lecture to accentuate a point, or at the end of a lecture to have students analyze and apply what they have just learned. Regardless of when you incorporate the game or activity, it is extremely important to let students know that what you are using to complement your lectures has been carefully curated to raise their thinking levels from the remembering levels to the evaluative and creative levels. Otherwise, students may think that you are experimenting on them or worst yet, that these activities are just for fun and no cognitive engagement is required.

8. Randomly Arrange Participants

I also make sure to use a number of ways to randomly arrange participants for group work to ensure all students have the opportunity to work with a variety of team members across the semester. It also allows students to relax and focus on the activity rather than having to find a partner for the activity or just engage with one other student they already know the whole semester. Among available strategies is the use of a grouping app or website. Many good apps and websites are available for randomly assigning groups such as Groupsort.com.

You can also simply have the participants count off by numbers through seven or try something fun such as having participants count off by "Mean, Median, Mode, and Standard Deviation, Upper Control Limit, Lower Control Limit, Range of Variation," for example. I have also used a deck of cards and had students sort by color, suit, or number that way.

9. Be Patient. Be Purposeful. Be Prepared.

Teaching, using games and activities, takes time to perfect. The one thing you cannot do is try and give up in despair. If you are used to only using lectures and videos, adding games and activities will surely take you out of your comfort zone. However, thanks to our brain's neuroplasticity, we all have the ability to modify, change, and adapt to new experiences. In other words, with practice, you will be able to "rewrite" your old patterns to improve your teaching. Why? Because lectures that are fun and engaging are far more likely to result in better outcomes, both in the short term and long term. You have the power to transform the classroom from a place you and the students *must* be to a place you and the students *want* to be.

To that end, I purposefully think of ways to creatively share with students a complicated concept or one that builds upon prior understanding. For example, I typically prepare a sandwich with all of the fixings to help students understand how we can ultimately take the cost of each part to determine how much we should charge for the sandwich. Then, I can help students understand where profit lies and the importance of knowing your costs as a business owner. I also use a puzzle to help students understand the importance of managers constantly painting the picture of where the company is headed and how their individual work (as a puzzle piece) is critical to the competition of the company objectives (or completion of the puzzle).

The fact of the matter is we are subject matter experts. Because of our knowledge and expertise, we are able to see and make sense of the world from our own perspectives. We are capable of bridging theory with practice. We can develop our praxis by using our current and past life experiences as the foundation and then we can wrap around the theories and the latest discoveries within our field to explain it to students. For example, the 1996 movie, *The Mirror Has Two Faces* depicts the lives of two middle-age Columbia University professors, Dr. Rose Morgan and Dr. Gregory Larkin, played masterfully by Barbara Streisand and Jeff Bridges (Streisand, 1996).

While the movie is about human connection and love, it is painfully evident that mathematics professor Dr. Larkin's dependency on lectures struggles to keep students awake, let alone engaged. On the other hand, literature professor Dr. Morgan uses her recent sister's wedding as the foundation to explain female literature archetypes. As she speaks of such experience, she brings humor and joy as part of the discussion. Additionally, even with a classroom of roughly sixty students, she is seen asking open-ended questions and calling on students by name. The energy in the class and the level of engagement by students and professors alike is palpable. Dr. Morgan creates powerful experiences for her students by bringing context and humor to her classroom.

A word of caution, however, if an activity is new to you, be flexible and modify it as you see it fitting best to your group of students. The worst thing that can happen is for you to become overwhelmed or discouraged. To prevent such negativity, make sure you are prepared and organized. Students are often tolerant of an activity not going as planned, but no one enjoys an activity that is poorly prepared.

10. Make Sure You Leave Enough Time to Debrief the Active Learning Activity

It is extremely important that you allow yourself and your students time to debrief and listen to one another's thoughts and perspectives. David Kolb, an American educational theorist and one of the forefathers of experiential education philosophy, believed that in order to truly learn from experience there must be time for reflection. In fact, debriefing is a core component of Kolb's Experiential Learning Cycle. By reflecting on and recognizing the knowledge, skills and attitudes used in an experience, participants develop personal awareness and insight and become aware of the inner resources they can access in future experiences. (Kolb, 1984)

Perhaps one of the most important aspect of games and activities is that they provide an opportunity for many discussion points. However, it is important to remember that if post-activity debriefs are not structured properly, they may not be effective and opportunities for learning may not surface.

In order to maximize the benefits of experiential activities and enable participants learning and development through the process, it's helpful to follow a three-step model for how to ask debrief questions: What? So What? Now What? (Schoel, Prouty, & Radcliffe, 1988).

Here are some notes about this process, directly from Schoel, Prouty, and Radcliffe's 1988 book *Islands of Healing: A Guide to Adventure Based Counselling*.

1. **The What?:**

Purpose: Review the activity to collect data of what happened

Explanation: The intention is to draw out as much information as possible from the group in order to refer back to it later on in the discussion. From this foundation of what happened, the facilitator can guide the discussion forward into greater understanding of the experience, and help draw out learning from it.

Example Questions: What happened? What took place during this activity? What did you observe?

2. **The So What?:**

Purpose: Look at details and interpret the data to draw out the significance of the activity in order to gain insight

Explanation: Moving from descriptive and observable to interpretive, the intention is to draw more meaning of what happened, and/or how it happened as well as to "unpack" the more subtle levels of what took place.

Example questions: How was your communication? What contributed to your team's success? What role did you play in the group during the activity?

3. **The Now What?:**

Purpose: Bridge from recent experience to future experience

Explanation: In order for what has just taken place to have significance or impact, the "now what" questions get the participants to think ahead and possibly apply what they have learnt. It may also be appropriate for participants to look at what has just taken place on a metaphoric level and draw meaning or insight in that way.

Note: On this last part of the debriefing, I sometimes incorporate Pause to Reflect (P2R) techniques where students are given five minutes to write a reflection of their learning without sharing their thoughts. I believe that using this technique helps students not only practice but also understand the power of reflection about what they are learning, how they are learning it, and identify places where they are confused and need more guidance.

After reading the above "how to," perhaps you may be thinking that these activities are similar to a Socratic seminar or Socratic classroom, and I wholeheartedly agree. In a similar fashion, these educational activities invite dialogue taking place in a powerful cooperative atmosphere where all participants work together to form share understandings. Educational games also require evidence and logic, engage the entire classroom to rise up above the definitions, and invite them to experience genuine human interaction where no participant gives up their identity but rather broadens their perspective.

I do want to emphasize that the use of educational games to augment the content is simply that—not a way to "entertain" students. Neil deGrasse Tyson, David Attenborough, and Carl Sagan were not clowns. The best teachers I have ever listened to were *passionate and able to explain complex subjects simply and intentionally.* Humor has its place, but I doubt it can incite passion for a subject. Appropriate humor in the classroom can provide a welcome reprieve, but it is no substitute for enthusiasm and good teaching skills. I believe that our role is to offer something meaningful, purposeful, and long-lasting. We do this by aiming to be genuinely relevant and engaging.

In watching the Disney/Pixar film *Luca*, directed by Enrico Casarosa, I found that the plot behind the film had some direct parallels with my views on teaching. In the film, we meet a "sea monster" longing to learn more about life outside of the sea. His sense of wonder takes him on an incredible adventure on land with Guilia, who is essentially a human underdog. Although most of the movie is based on the trials and tribulations experienced by Luca, where he tries to conquer the human world while keeping his true identity a secret, there is a moment when Luca shares with Guilia what he learned from Alberto, his "sea monster" friend, of the world beyond the ocean. Guilia gently and kindly informs Luca of the realities of the world. She never said, "you are wrong." She generously shared her knowledge unconditionally, and Lucas discovered his passion for learning. My hope in sharing this is to let us all change our perspectives and create an environment so that every one of our students is inspired to learn more, think bigger, and accomplish things they never thought possible (Casarosa, 2020).

PART TWO:

READY TO USE GAMES

INTRODUCTION TO GAME SECTION

What I have learned the most from incorporating educational games into my lectures is that teaching becomes more exciting and enjoyable. Students reciprocate the effort, bringing in enthusiasm and a true desire to learn and engage in conversations, often leading to deeper understanding. I have found the more I use educational games, the more they become the backbone to a successful approach to teaching. Additionally, and perhaps most importantly, educational activities allow each student, regardless of background, to see themselves as contributors and good students, whereas memorizing information and reciting it back is no longer the rule nor the expectation.

In the pages that follow, you will find a collection of simple and valuable educational games you can use to instruct a variety of topics. All of these games and activities are grounded on Kolb's (1984) model of experiential learning focused on providing students with: 1) concrete experiences, 2) reflection/observation, 3) abstract conception, and 4) active experimentation (Kolb, 1984).

Keep in mind, a single activity can be used to teach more than a single subject or principle. Explore and experiment to fit the activity to your learning objectives. One common theme among this collection is you will not need a substantial amount of training budget to replicate these activities. In many cases, you will find the materials you need already in the faculty stationary closet or in your pantry.

ICEBREAKERS

In the icebreaker section, you will find a sample of activities you can use for the first day of class. Those games allow students to relax, as it is normal to feel out-of-place or nervous about how they will come across to others. Icebreakers are intended to help people get to know each other and become more comfortable with each other, as your goal is to have them communicate, learn, and work better together. These icebreakers also allow you as a professor to invite students to elaborate, ask questions, and get to know them a bit more before class begins. These games have allowed me to also learn my students' names much faster on the first day of school.

SKILL BUILDING:

In the skill building section, you will find games and activities intended to engage your students' core competencies such as communication, teamwork, perspective, and empathy. These games allow students to demonstrate independence, comprehend as well as critique, value evidence, understand other perspectives, and build strong content knowledge.

FOCUSED

In the focused section, you will find activities that will help you creatively teach concepts in science, engineering, math, or really any subject matter. For example, one activity helps students understand why the methodology section of a research project is so important or the significance of going through an iterative process to achieve better outcomes.

I respectfully invite you to try to find the right balance for you between lectures and educational activities. Having fun while you teach is energizing and delightful. You will quickly find yourself knowing students as individuals better, become better at reflective practicing and listening skills, and invite them to develop a sense of wonder and curiosity which can last forever.

ICEBREAKERS:

THE STORY OF YOUR NAME

I'M AN ACRONYM

I'M IMPRESSED

COMMONALITIES

WHICH WOULD YOU RATHER

WHODUNIT

GAME: THE STORY OF YOUR NAME

PURPOSE/OBJECTIVES:

This is a great activity where students are invited to share a little bit about their own name, providing insights about their family history. It is a great activity to have students reflect on their own and each other's background and to build classroom community.

GROUP SIZE: Between 15–20.

MATERIALS: Index Cards. Timer.

TIME: 30–40 minutes.

PRE-WORK:

On a whiteboard or easel board, write the following prompt questions. Do not allow students to see it until after you have provided the instructions.

- Does your name have a meaning?
- Who else in your family do you share your name with or who were you named after?
- Do you like your name?
- Do people sometimes mispronounce or misspell your name? If so, how?
- Is there a story connected to your name?

PROCEDURE:

Distribute the index cards and ask students to spend the next five to eight minutes thinking more closely about their name and write answers to any one or all of the following questions on the index card provided. Have the students write their first and last name on the back of the card and request students turn in their cards at the end of the class session.

After five to eight minutes, begin with you, as the facilitator, sharing the story of your name. This will help students feel more at ease sharing their stories and will allow you to begin sharing interesting facts about you. After you share, provide each student an opportunity to share their own story about their name. Provide about a minute or two per student. I find some students really enjoy this exercise and share stories about themselves and their families while other students are more factual and just share who else has the same name in their families. Regardless of the amount of sharing, I make sure to thank students for sharing their story with me and the class.

TIPS:

This activity will greatly enhance your ability to learn *and* remember your students' name and will also serve as a quick way to take attendance after class.

Adapted from:
Scannell, M., & Cain, J. (2012). Puzzles and Games with Teachable Moments. In *Big Book of Low-Cost Training Games: Quick, Effective Activities that Encourage Out-of-the-Box Thinking, Improve Collaboration, and Spark Great Ideas!* (1st ed., p. 37). New York, NY: McGraw Hill.

GAME: I'M AN ACRONYM

PURPOSE/OBJECTIVE:

This is a great activity where students are invited to share a little bit about themselves using their name as an acronym. It is a great activity to have students reflect on their own personal characteristics/uniqueness.

GROUP SIZE: Between 15–20.

MATERIALS: Index Cards. Timer.

TIME: 20–30 minutes.

PROCEDURE:

Distribute the index cards and ask students to spend the next five to eight minutes thinking more closely about their name and think of it as an acronym (the name can be their first or middle name). For example, SILVIA could be Special, Intelligent, Loyal, Vacations, Interesting, Adaptable (it is best when the facilitator uses their own name as an example). Share a little about why each word has a meaning in your life or personality.

Instruct the students to write their own acronym on the index card provided. Have the students write their first and last name on the back of the card and request students turn in their cards at the end of the class session.

After five to eight minutes, begin having students share their acronym. Make positive comments or ask questions as students share their acronyms to help them get used to speaking in the classroom.

TIPS:

This activity will greatly enhance your ability to learn/remember your students' name and will also serve as a quick way to take attendance after class.

Adapted from:

Scannell, M., & Cain, J. (2012). Puzzles and Games with Teachable Moments. In *Big Book of Low-Cost Training Games: Quick, Effective Activities that Encourage Out-of-the-Box Thinking, Improve Collaboration, and Spark Great Ideas!* (1st ed., p. 23). New York, NY: McGraw Hill.

GAME: I'M IMPRESSED

PURPOSE/OBJECTIVE:

This is a great activity where students are invited to use their creativity and imagination. It is a fun activity to have students meet one another.

GROUP SIZE: Between 20–30.

MATERIALS: Index Cards. Timer.

TIME: 25–35 minutes.

PROCEDURE:

Distribute the index cards and ask students to work with the person next to them (either to the right, left or behind them). Instruct the pairs of students to work together and come up with three statements each to be shared with the whole class. The objective of the statements is to make everyone be so very impressed.

For example, as the facilitator, pair up with another student and say, "I would like to introduce to you David. I just learned he is one of the engineers working at SpaceX designing the new homes to be built in Mars. Because of his job, he travels back and forth to Mars every ten years. Most impressively, David has never been detected as an impostor in the game, Among Us."

Instruct students to write their three statements on their own index card and write their names on the back. Share with students that you will collect the cards at the end class (which will serve to help take attendance). Provide them with eight to ten minutes to work between partners. Encourage them to be creative. Have the pair of students trade cards so the pair can introduce each other. As students introduce each other, ask questions about their statements to encourage creativity and fluidity of expression.

Adapted from:
Scannell, M., & Cain, J. (2012). Puzzles and Games with Teachable Moments. In *Big Book of Low-Cost Training Games: Quick, Effective Activities that Encourage Out-of-the-Box Thinking, Improve Collaboration, and Spark Great Ideas!* (1st ed., p. 135). New York, NY: McGraw Hill

GAME: COMMONALITIES

PURPOSE/OBJECTIVE:

This is a great group activity where students are invited to use their creativity to determine which group has the most things in common. It is a fun activity to have students meet one another.

GROUP SIZE: Between 20–30.

MATERIALS: Timer.

TIME: 20–30 minutes.

PROCEDURE:

Break students into teams of up to five. Try to split them in fun ways. For example, grab an old deck of playing cards. Pass them out to the entire group. Split the students by suit, number, or color.

Once the students are in groups, tell them they have ten minutes to work together to determine at least ten things they have in common. Obvious things like gender, hair color, or body parts do not count. Each team will have to get creative and get to talking to learn at least ten things all students share in common before the other teams do (or before the clock runs out).

At the end of game, each team will reveal their commonalities to the larger group. As a facilitator, you determine which team wins between the one that finishes first and/or the one that finds the most commonalities.

GAME: WHICH WOULD YOU RATHER

PURPOSE/OBJECTIVE:

This is a great activity where students are invited to answer a question and explain their answer to the group. It is a fun activity to have students meet one another.

GROUP SIZE: Between 20–30.

MATERIALS: Handout of Would You Rather Questions.

ALTERNATIVE: Cut out each of the questions and place them in a container. Randomly take out one question per student.

Note: If there are more than thirty-five students, you can develop your own questions or repeat the questions provided.

TIME: 20–30 minutes.

PROCEDURE:

Tell students they each will have to introduce themselves by sharing their name and where they are from. After they share this information, you will be asking them a random "would you rather" question. Each student is to answer the question and provide a short explanation as to why they chose that particular option. Have fun by asking some follow up questions if necessary.

ALTERNATIVE:

Tell students they each will have to introduce themselves by sharing their name and where they are from. After they share this information, you will be asking them to pull out a "would you rather" question from a container. Each student is to answer the question and provide a short explanation as to why they chose that particular option. Have fun by asking some follow up questions if necessary.

HANDOUT:

1. Would you rather: Have to listen to Nickelback or Maroon 5 for the rest of your life?
2. Would you rather: Live in a penthouse in a big city or in a bungalow on the beach?
3. Would you rather: Always have to say every single thing you think or never be able to speak again?
4. Would you rather: Have the hiccups for the rest of your life or always feel like you have to sneeze (without actually sneezing)?
5. Would you rather: Be famous when you're alive, but forgotten after you die or unknown when you're alive, but famous for forever after?
6. Would you rather: Be able to see the future or be able to redo the past?
7. Would you rather: Be swelteringly hot or be artic cold?
8. Would you rather: Be able to fly or be able to breathe underwater?
9. Would you rather: Be able to fly anywhere for free anytime you wanted or have your tab permanently covered at all restaurants?
10. Would you rather: Have 8 a.m. classes every day or 8 p.m. classes every day?
11. Would you rather: Have a job you hated that made you rich or have a job you loved that ensured you would always be poor?
12. Would you rather: Never be able to eat desserts again or never be able to sleep in again?

13. Would you rather: Never have a smartphone again or never have a laptop again?
14. Would you rather: Have tickets to every school's football game or every school basketball game?
15. Would you rather: Be able to eat anywhere for free or be able to get any clothes from any store for free?
16. Would you rather: Have the worst professor of all time once or have just okay professors forever?
17. Would you rather: Not be able to taste or not be able to see colors?
18. Would you rather: Have to sing everything you say (but say as much as you want), or talk normally but only be allowed one hundred words a day?
19. Would you rather: Be a famous politician or a reality TV star?
20. Would you rather: Have a constantly messy dorm room or a constantly smelly dorm room?
21. Would you rather: Be the smartest person of all time or the most beautiful person of all time?
22. Would you rather: Get a degree in what you love or get a degree in something that will make you money?
23. Would you rather: Be able to time travel, but not control what time you go to or be able to teleport but not be able to control where you go?
24. Would you rather: Be a famous actor or a famous singer?
25. Would you rather: Lose your wallet once a year and have to replace everything in it or lose your phone once a year and have to replace it?

26. Would you rather: Live in the world of *Harry Potter* or the world of *Star Wars*?

27. Would you rather: Be convicted for life for a crime you didn't commit or have someone else serve a life sentence for a crime you committed?

28. Would you rather: Have to ride a horse everywhere you go or have to ride a bus everywhere you go?

29. Would you rather: Be poor in the world of today or rich, but live two thousand years ago?

30. Would you rather: Have only terrible and boring professors but get all As or have great and interesting professors but get all Cs?

31. Would you rather: Only be able to listen to one of the songs you love for the rest of your life or be able to listen to any of the songs that you hate for the rest of your life?

32. Would you rather: Have it always be summer or always be winter?

33. Would you rather: Have everyone not believe anything you say or have everything you say be broadcast to the entire world?

34. Would you rather: Be the best in the world at a sport no one cares about or have an average career playing a very popular sport?

35. Would you rather: Drink coffee or a sport energy drink?

GAME: WHODUNIT

PURPOSE/OBJECTIVE:

This is a simple guessing game where students are invited to share one fact about themselves. It is a fun activity to have students meet one another.

GROUP SIZE: BETWEEN 20–30.

MATERIALS: INDEX CARDS.

TIME: 20–30 MINUTES.

PROCEDURE:

Separate the students into groups of six to ten. Have each person in the group write down on the index card one thing they have done in life that most people would not necessarily guess. For example, I have had students say the wildest things such as "I was a finalist in American Idol" or "I found a dead body while fishing with a friend" (and they were true!). Then, put the index cards for each group in a hat and shuffle it up. Pass the hat around, have each participant draw an index card, and try to guess which group member did that thing. Select a participant, have him/her read the index card, and provide three opportunities to correctly guess "whodunit." If the participant is unable to guess correctly, have the person "whodunit" reveal who they are to the group and share more about the fact. Students have a lot of fun trying to guess "whodunit."

ALTERNATIVE:

If the group of students does not exceed twenty, have all index cards go into one hat. As the facilitator, pull one card at a time, read it, and select a student who will have three attempts to successfully identify "whodunit." If the student is unable to guess correctly, have the person "whodunit" reveal who they are to the group.

SKILL BUILDING:

LET'S COMMUNICATE

BUILD A JIGSAW PUZZLE

MARSHMALLOW AND SPAGHETTI TOWER

MODERN HIEROGLYPHICS

KEEP OR FIRE THE CEO

THE CURSE OF KNOWLEDGE LINK

POWERFUL PATTERNS

FRACTURED T

BALL POINT GAME

THE CASE OF TWO BALLOONS

GAME: LET'S COMMUNICATE

PURPOSE/OBJECTIVES:

1) Understand the challenges of interpersonal communication.
2) Understand communication issues within organizations.
3) Understand the importance of communicating clearly and effectively.

GROUP SIZE: Any.

MATERIALS: One sheet of copy paper for each student.

TIME: 8–10 minutes.

PROCEDURE:

Provide a sheet of paper to each student. As you are distributing the paper, ask the students to stand. Share with them that you will be providing them with verbal instructions on what to do with the sheet of paper.

Once all students are standing up with the sheet of paper on their hands, ask them to close their eyes and then you say, "You must follow each of my instructions. You are not allowed to ask any questions. Fold the paper in half and tear off the lower right corner and the top left corner. Fold the paper in half again and tear off the top left corner. Open your eyes and hold your paper so everyone can see it."

It is very likely that the student's papers will be different from each other.

DISCUSSION QUESTIONS:

- Why did we end up with different results?
- Would it have helped to have your eyes open? Why? Why not?
- How does this game relate to our lecture on communication?

SUGGESTED LECTURE TOPICS:

- Communication process, methods, and barriers
- Manager's role in communicating decisions to employees
- Active Listening

STUDENT LEARNING OBJECTIVES:

- Acquire an integrative understanding of the importance of communication in management and leadership.

Understand and develop ways to overcome communication barriers.

A LITTLE SAMPLE OF A LECTURE DISCUSSION:

Communication is crucial to organizational performance. Communication is not just about talking; it is about forming connections with other people. Perhaps, one of the most powerful benefits of communication is found in employee engagement. Employees who clearly understand what is expected of them and who find evidence that their input is being heard can better align with company objectives. A manager can improve employee engagement through communication in the following ways:

- Find out what motivates and fulfills the employee.
- Have a better understanding of employee's talents and skills.

- Improve the connection between coworkers for a more positive and satisfying work environment.

Adapted from:
Scannell, M., & Cain, J. (2012). Puzzles and Games with Teachable Moments. In *Big Book of Low-Cost Training Games: Quick, Effective Activities that Explore Communication, Goal Setting, Character Development, Teambuilding, and more* (1st ed., p. 97). New York, NY: McGraw Hill

GAME: BUILD A JIGSAW PUZZLE

PURPOSE/OBJECTIVES:

1) Understand the power and the responsibility of the leader to clearly communicate the mission or task at hand.
2) Create community and collaborative relationships within the classroom.

GROUP SIZE: Groups of 3–4.

MATERIALS: A variety of fifty- or one-hundred-piece jigsaw puzzles. An index card and a pen per group.

TIME: 25–30 minutes.

PROCEDURE:

Place puzzles randomly at each table making sure the puzzle's image is not revealed. Advise students to start working on the puzzles and encourage them to work in groups of three to four. Play upbeat music to create an inviting and jovial environment. After ten minutes, stop the activity and have each group give a brief description of what they believe their jigsaw puzzle is about and write it on a piece of paper. Then, allow the teams to return to the activity for the remainder of the time allotted to the activity (maximum thirty minutes).

Variations

If time permits, invite students to walk around the room and interpret the other team's puzzles. Have participants write on the paper their own interpretation of the puzzle's image.

DISCUSSION QUESTIONS:

- Would it have helped to know the image of the jigsaw puzzle?
- What is the benefit of knowing the image before engaging in solving the puzzle?
- What are different things the puzzle could represent?

SUGGESTED LECTURE TOPICS:

- Manager's job and responsibility in sharing the mission to employees
- Leader's responsibility to determine if the mission remains relevant
- Power and importance of a company's mission statement
- Alignment of employees' personal values and company's mission statement

STUDENT LEARNING OBJECTIVES:

- Acquire an integrative understanding of management and leadership.
- Develop the ability to analyze and evaluate the importance of clearly communicating the mission as a strategic initiative.
- Further examine management and leadership.

A LITTLE SAMPLE OF A LECTURE DISCUSSION:

At the onset of this activity, I trusted that you already knew how to complete a jigsaw puzzle. I also trusted that if you did not know or could not remember well enough, you would ask me or ask someone within the group to mentor you to learn the skill. As a new manager in the workplace, you will have to trust your employees will come with the desired skills to the table. Rather than questioning or inspecting the employee's skill level, a great manager devotes all of his/her time, energy, and skill to communicate and paint the picture (i.e., the company's mission) through their words and actions to their employees thus creating a fertile ground for success.

I learned early on from one of my management professors that you have to live by three rules: 1) you tell your employees the mission, 2) you tell them you told them, and 3) you tell them again, as it is easy for people to forget about the mission in the midst of day-to-day activities. This philosophy is not about mindless, empty repetition of boilerplate soundbites. Hammering the same audience with the same message using the same words repeatedly is a recipe for being tuned out. Instead, it is really about cultivating awareness of and buy-in for the mission, so it is more like a practiced persistence. After all, for managers and leaders alike, it is all about improving the lives of those whom they have been entrusted to lead.

OTHER POTENTIAL APPLICATIONS:

This game has been successfully used in a grant writing class to help illustrate the importance of painting a clear picture through the details of a grant application.

This game could also serve to help students understand how important it is to choose a company to work for whose "picture" is one they personally like and feel proud of speaking about to others. Finding true alignment of personal values to the company's mission is critical to the company's success and their own personal and professional success.

Created by: Dr. Silviana Falcon

GAME: MARSHMALLOW AND SPAGHETTI TOWER

PURPOSE:

Understanding the importance of planning, teamwork, innovation, motivation, creativity.

GROUP SIZE: Any; split teams into groups of 3 or 4.

MATERIALS:

One package of spaghetti. One bag of large marshmallows. One bag of small marshmallows. One box of large Ziploc bags. A ruler or tape measure. Legal-size paper.

TIME: 30 minutes.

PRE-GAME PROCEDURE:

In each large Ziploc bag, place precisely thirty pieces of spaghetti, ten small marshmallows, and one large marshmallow. Each team will get one bag, so create as many bags as you think you will need depending on the group size.

GAME PROCEDURE:

Split students into smaller work teams of three to four students each. Once the teams are created, give each team one of the Ziploc bags containing the marshmallows and spaghetti. Also, provide each team a legal-size paper to serve as the foundation for each tower. This will also help to quickly remove and trash the tower once the game is completed. Tell the students they have fifteen minutes to build the highest freestanding tower they can to support the weight of the large marshmallow, using only the building supplies contained in the Ziploc bag. The tower must be able to stand on its own without tipping over.

Play lively music as students work. After fifteen minutes, call time. Have fun with the testing (controlling phase). Make a big production. Go around each structure, building suspense and drama as you measure the towers slowly.

DISCUSSION QUESTIONS:

- What was the most challenging part of building this tower?
- What was your team's approach to the build?
- Did you make any changes to your approach along the way?
- Did your team find inspiration or ideas from other teams?
- Did the competition motivate you?

SUGGESTED LECTURE TOPICS:

- Planning as a method to set direction
- Planning as a method to reduce uncertainty, waste, and redundancy
- Planning as a method to establish goals and standards

STUDENT LEARNING OBJECTIVES:

Understand the nature and purpose of planning.

A LITTLE SAMPLE OF A LECTURE DISCUSSION:

It is common human behavior not wanting to let a problem linger for long. We want to get rid of it as soon as possible. Hence, we start doing without planning the actions and their possible consequences. We repeat mistakes of the past or create new problems from our own solutions. Ever wondered why some people solve problems more effectively than most? They look at a problem from different angles and plan. Albert Einstein understood the importance of planning when he said, *"If I had an hour to solve a problem, I'd spend 55 minutes thinking about the problem and 5 minutes thinking about solutions"* (Kat aria, 2014).

Adapted from:
Scannell, M., & Cain, J. (2012). Puzzles and Games with Teachable Moments. In *Big Book of Low-Cost Training Games: Quick, Effective Activities that Encourage Out-of-the-Box Thinking, Improve Collaboration, and Spark Great Ideas!* (1st ed., p. 135). New York, NY: McGraw Hill

Citation:
Kataria, Vishal. "3 Things About Problem Solving Which Albert Einstein Teaches Us." LinkedIn, June 9, 2014.

https://www.linkedin.com/pulse/20140609042202-59384553-3-things-about-problem
solving-which-albert-einstein-teaches-us/

GAME: MODERN HIEROGLYPHICS

Hidden Meaning. Looking beyond what is in front of us.

PURPOSE/OBJECTIVES:

1) Understand the responsibility of the leader to seek solutions by seeing the world from a different perspective.
2) Foster innovative thinking.
3) Look at problems from a different perspective.
4) Create community and collaborative relationships within the classroom.

GROUP SIZE: Any.

MATERIALS: Pencils. A copy of the Modern Hieroglyphics Handout.

TIME: 10–15 minutes.

PROCEDURE:

Provide a pencil and a copy of the puzzle handout to each participant. Encourage students to review each puzzle carefully, looking for patterns. Each puzzle has a meaning, and their job is to decipher it. They can write what they think it means at the bottom of each picture. I suggest playing game soundtracks such as Jeopardy or classical music to set up a joyful environment and lower the stress level of the students.

Provide the students five minutes to review on their own. After five minutes, ask them to pair up with the person next to them and share their findings. Provide them five minutes to compare and work together on deciphering the words. After ten minutes, stop the activity. Go in order of pictures starting with number one. Ask for volunteers to speak up and share what they deciphered. Celebrate their correct answers or ingenuity.

Variations

If time permits, invite participants to try out innovative thinking. I typically allow another ten minutes to have students come up with their own hieroglyphics and share among themselves.

DISCUSSION QUESTIONS:

- Did you find this exercise easy or hard? Why? Why not?
- Did it get easier as the answers were being given?
- Was it hard to develop your own hieroglyphics?
- How does this game relate to our lecture of management?

SUGGESTED LECTURE TOPICS:

- Manager's role in problem solving
- Manager's role in innovation
- Power and importance of critical thinking
- Creativity and innovation

STUDENT LEARNING OBJECTIVES:

- Examine and (re)define a problem by involving different perspectives.
- Apply current understanding to develop innovative (creative) solutions.

- Engage the imagination to explore new possibilities.
- Formulate and articulate ideas.
- Weigh connections and relationships.
- Engage the imagination to explore new possibilities.
- Reason toward a conclusion or application.

A LITTLE SAMPLE OF A LECTURE DISCUSSION:

Most solutions are hidden within the problem. The critical role of the manager is to untangle the symptoms from the problem. Once the problem is clearly identified, the solution is typically hidden within it. Just like in this exercise, one must learn to look at the problem from a different perspective.

Adapted from:
Scannell, M., & Cain, J. (2012). Puzzles and Games with Teachable Moments. In *Big Book of Low-Cost Training Games: Quick, Effective Activities that Explore Communication, Goal Setting, Character Development, Teambuilding, and* (1st ed., p. 163). New York, NY: McGraw Hill

DECODE THE HIDDEN MEANING

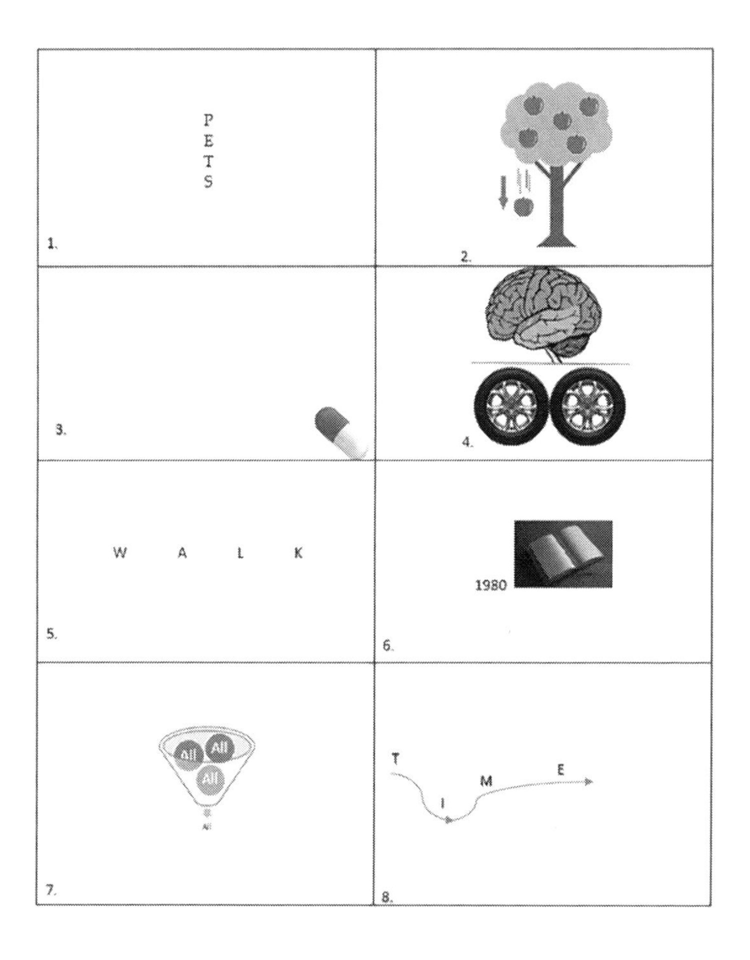

DECODE THE HIDDEN MEANING

ANSWERS:

1. Step up

2. The apple never falls far from the tree

3. Pillow

4. Smart car

5. Long walk

6. Yearbook

7. All in

8. Time flies

GAME: KEEP OR FIRE THE CEO

PURPOSE/OBJECTIVES:

1) Understand how external circumstances or factors beyond a manager's control can affect the success or failure of an organization.
2) Understand the omnipotent and symbolic views of management theory.

GROUP SIZE: Any.

MATERIALS: Board or easel pad. One regular deck of playing cards.

TIME: 20–30 minutes.

PRE-GAME PROCEDURE:

1. Remove the Joker card as it will not be needed for this game.
2. Create four distinct stacks of cards by taking one card from each suit in ascending order. For example: first stack: 1 of clubs, 2 of diamonds, 3 of hearts, 4 of spades, 5 of clubs, 6 of diamonds, 7 of hearts, 8 of spades, 9 of clubs, 10 of diamonds, King of clubs, Queen of diamonds, Jack of hearts, and an Ace of spades. Repeat the above sequence starting with the 1 of diamonds. **The main goal** is to avoid having two consecutive numbers of the same suit within each of the new four stacks.

PROCEDURE:

Start by randomly assigning students into four separate groups. Once students are in their respective groups, ask them to select one team member who will be their chief executive officer. This person will be responsible for the success or failure of their team. Tell the teams that the CEO with the most points will win. To create excitement, consider offering a reward to the winning team (like extra credit).

While the teams select their CEO, place the four distinct pre-arranged stacks on a table positioned in a way that all four teams can see (toward the front of the classroom tends to be best). Ask each team to share three to four reasons as to why they selected the person as their CEO (e.g., credibility within the team, friendliness, trustworthiness, etc.).

Invite the four CEOs to the table where the playing cards are stacked and ask each to stand by any one of the four playing card stacks. Once they have selected their stack, share the following rules:

1. Each of you will have three distinct trials to pull three cards from your selected stack of cards.
2. The cards must remain face down.
3. The goal is to select three cards that are of the same suit and the three cards must be in order (e.g., 3, 4, 5 of hearts).
4. Each of you can (and should) shuffle your selected stack of cards to increase the odds of being successful.
5. Each of you can engage their team in terms of what strategy to follow in selecting the three cards (e.g., every other

one, last three, top three, middle three) or they can execute based on their own strategy as they are the selected CEO.

6. The team with the most successes receives x number of points (for extra credit or small token for each team participant).

7.) If there is a tie, an extra trial will be played. The team with most successes wins.

To create a fun atmosphere, allow a couple of minutes for the CEOs and each of their teams to talk about and plan their strategy. After three to four minutes, bring the CEOs back to the table and ask them to select their three cards and share their outcome with the entire group of students.

After the first trial, write each team's performance on the board or easel pad, making sure it is visible to all teams (success/failures by trial by team). Since the cards are stacked against them, they will all receive a failure mark.

Conduct the second trial in the same fashion; however, this time **change one of the rules.** The team can be successful if they **pick three cards that are sequential regardless of the suit** (This change will increase the odds of having a winning team this round). Have the CEOs share their selection with the entire group of students. Write the success or failure outcome for the second trial on the board/easel creating excitement and a competitive environment.

Before conducting the third trial, ask the CEOs to leave the room. Once the four CEOs exit, ask the teams if they think their CEO is the right person for the job. They have the option to keep or fire their CEO. Inform them that they only have one more trial left to earn the extra credit or the token and, so far, they have all been close but unsuccessful (or only one or two teams have been successful). If they choose to keep or fire their CEO, they must provide one to two reasons as to why they will keep or fire their CEO. If a team decides to fire the CEO, ask them to appoint a new CEO who could be from their own team or from another team. The team that selects a new CEO must provide reasoning for selecting the new person who will act as their new CEO. Allow the teams five minutes to make a decision.

Ask each team to share with all of the students their decision to either keep or fire their CEO. Summarize the one to two reasons behind each team's decision to either keep their CEO or fire and hire a new CEO and write it on the board.

Bring back the CEOs, share with them the question posted to each team and each of the team's decision to either keep, fire, and replace them as their leader (Have as much fun on this section and ensure that the comments are not personal or demeaning).

Conduct the third trial. This time, the CEOs (either from before or newly appointed) must select three cards of the same suit in sequential order (same as in trial #1). Have each CEO present their selection to their team and all students as before. Write the outcome on the board by team.

DISCUSSION QUESTIONS:

- What happened? Why was it so hard to have the teams be successful (this is where you may want to share that the odds were stacked against success as the environment (cards) had been manipulated in such a way to decrease their odds of being successful)?

- Did the team's culture have anything to do with the decision to keep or fire and hire a new CEO?
- What factors could have contributed to the failure?
- What else could the teams have done to increase the opportunity for success?
- What are the key issues?
- How does this activity relate to the constraints and challenges experienced by corporate leaders?
- What would you do differently next time?
- What did you learn?
- Was this experience worthwhile?

SUGGESTED LECTURE TOPICS:

- Organization's external environment and corporate culture
- Omnipotent and symbolic view of management
- Mergers and acquisitions

STUDENT LEARNING OBJECTIVES:

- Evaluate and differentiate the omnipotent and symbolic views of management.
- Appraise the constraints and challenges facing managers.
- Evaluate the characteristics and analyze the importance of organizational culture.

A LITTLE SAMPLE OF A LECTURE DISCUSSION:

Managers are extremely important to the success or failure of an organization. Excellent managers are capable of anticipating change, seizing opportunities, and implementing innovative solutions to respond to the ever-changing external environment. When a company's profits increase, managers are often rewarded with bonuses and/or stock options. When there is a decline in profits, managers are often the first to be replaced in favor for someone new who can lead the company to success.

This thinking aligns with the omnipotent view of management theory, where the manager is viewed as a take-charge type of business executive who can overcome any obstacle. This view is prevalent across industries in countries such as the United States. For example, it explains turnover among sport coaches, as they are considered the "managers" of their teams if their teams are under performing. A new coach is expected to correct poor performance.

The symbolic view, on the other hand, argues that managers are not all that powerful, and, thus, the organization's success or failure is determined by external forces outside their control. Managers simply symbolize control and influence by developing plans to respond to the external constraints. The organization's culture heavily influences whether it responds from an omnipotent or a symbolic view of management.

Developed by:
Dr. Silviana Falcon

GAME: THE CURSE OF KNOWLEDGE LINK

INTRODUCTION:

This game is the result of Dr. Elizabeth Newton's dissertation work at Stanford University in 1990. In her dissertation, Dr. Newton assigned people to one of two roles: "tappers" or "listeners." Each tapper picks out a song from a list provided and taps out the rhythm to the listener by knocking on the table. We are going to reproduce her dissertation activity.

PURPOSE/OBJECTIVES:

1) Understanding how knowledge can prevent clear communication.
2) Experience how distractions (organizational noise) can negatively impact performance.
3) Understand the importance of clear communication.

GROUP SIZE: Any.

MATERIALS: Tapper and Listeners Handout. A timer.

TIME: 20–30 minutes.

MUSIC: None.

PROCEDURE:

Break students into pairs. Share with students that they will have one of two roles: "tapper" or "listener." The tappers will be tapping out popular tunes on the table, and the listeners will have to guess what the tune is. Provide a couple of minutes for students to determine their role. Once the tappers are identified, give them a copy of a list of twenty-five popular tunes, such as "Happy Birthday" and "Jingle Bells." Request that the tapper read the instructions silently. Allow a couple of minutes for the tapper to read.

Step 1: This step requires the tapper to predict the probability of the listeners being able to guess the song correctly. Do not share the prediction information.

Step 2: Once this step is completed, the tapper has to tap out the tune with their fingers on a table and the partner who is the listener has to guess the song.

DISCUSSION QUESTIONS:

By the way, listeners, one thing I did not mention before, the tappers were charged with one more task. Before they tapped the song to you, they were to predict if you were going to be able to accurately tell the name of the song. So, tappers, how did the listeners do?

- Raise your hand if you were a tapper? COUNT.
- How many of you predicted that your listener would accurately name the song? COUNT.
- How many of you actually predicted correctly? COUNT.

1. Tappers:

Did you experience any problems tapping?

Could you hear the tune in your head?

What factors contributed to your listener's success or failure at identifying the tunes?

2. Listeners:

What factors contributed to your success or failure at identifying the tunes?

What else could your tapper have done to increase the opportunity for success?

3. All students:

How does this activity relate to the constraints and challenges experienced in communication?

What would you do differently next time?

What did you learn?

Was this experience worthwhile?

SUGGESTED LECTURE TOPICS:

- Overcoming communication barriers
- he interpersonal communication process
- Organizational communication
- Becoming better communicators
- Organizational Noise

STUDENT LEARNING OBJECTIVES:

- Analyze the nature and function of effective communication.
- Appraise the challenges in interpersonal communication.
- Analyze the importance of effective listening.
- Formulate methods to overcome barriers to communication.

A LITTLE SAMPLE OF A LECTURE DISCUSSION:

Tapping the song was easy, guessing the tune was a really difficult task. In Dr. Newton's experiment, the success rate of the listener guessing the correct name to the tune being tapped was 2.5 percent. Interestingly, the tappers predicted a 50 percent success rate by the listener (Heath and Heath, 2007).

Therefore, what do we conclude from this study (Actually, what makes this study worthy of a dissertation)? What we find out is that the listener's job is quite difficult. When a tapper taps, she is hearing the song in her head. Meanwhile, the listeners cannot hear the tune. All they hear is a bunch of disconnected taps.

Is it hard to be the tapper? The problem is that the tappers have the knowledge (the song title) and that makes it hard or nearly impossible for them to imagine what it is like for the listener. Our knowledge has "cursed us."

Moreover, what about the listener? Well, not only does she not have the tune playing in her head, but there are other people tapping everywhere, making it hard to focus. This results in utter frustration.

The tapper/listener experiment is reenacted every day across the world. The tappers and listeners are the CEOs and frontline employees, teachers and students, politicians and voters, marketers, and customers. So how do you beat the villain?

TAKEAWAYS:

1. As leaders, we often fall into the tapper's trap! We have the knowledge about our strategy clearly in our heads, but it may not be as clear to our followers.
2. If you experience a problem stemming from lack of communication, start by assessing the tapper—not the listener.
3. Practice something the military knows well: 1) Tell them, 2) Tell them that you told them, 3) Tell them again.
4. Tapping louder or tapping repeatedly makes no difference to the listener.

Citation:
Heath, Chip, and Dan Heath. *Made to stick: Why some ideas survive and others die*. Random House, 2007.

Adapted by:
Dr. Silviana Falcon

TAPPER AND LISTENERS HANDOUT

Elizabeth Newton, PhD in Psychology (Stanford University)
Tappers and Listeners Study (1990)

Instructions:

As a tapper, your job is to pick out a song from the list provided and tap out the rhythm to a listener (by knocking on the desk/table). Your partner is the listener. Their job is to guess the song, based on the rhythm being tapped. BEFORE you tap the song, take a minute and make a prediction. Decide ahead of time if you think your listener will accurately name the song.

Song	Prediction Y/N	Outcome Y/N
"Happy Birthday To You"		
"The Star-Spangled Banner"		
"Itsy Bitsy Spider"		
"If You Are Happy And You Know It"		
"Bingo"		
"Somewhere Over the Rainbow"		
"Rudolph the Red-Nosed Reindeer"		
"Mary Had a Little Lamb"		
"Twinkle, Twinkle Little Star"		
"Jingle Bells"		
"The London Bridge		

Students' Names:

Listener: ____

Tapper: ____

GAME: POWERFUL PATTERNS

INTRODUCTION:

Pattern recognition is powerful because it can lead to new discoveries, breakthrough ideas, and innovative thinking. This game allows students to see the importance of having an open mind, being creative and analytical, and problem solving, which are all necessary skills to develop critical thinking skills.

PURPOSE/OBJECTIVE:

Critical thinking is a dynamic process that can be improved by practicing different ways of drawing reasonable conclusions from a set of information. This activity helps students begin exercising problem solving and creativity muscles.

GROUP SIZE: Any.

MATERIALS: Patterns Handout.

TIME: 15–20 minutes.

PROCEDURE:

Give the group members the patterns handout and instruct them to work on it independently for four to five minutes. After five minutes, ask them to work with the person (s) next to them and share ideas on how to solve the puzzles. Provide them another two to three minutes to work together. Then, ask for solutions for any of the puzzles. Have some fun facilitating this brainstorming session. After a couple of minutes, help the team solve Puzzle #1. Encourage them to work on the remaining solutions.

DISCUSSION QUESTIONS:

- How does this activity relate to how we can develop our creativity and critical thinking skills?
- Was it helpful to know the solution to the first question to know the solution to the second one?
- Did you adapt your thinking?
- What did you learn?
- Was this experience worthwhile?

SUGGESTED LECTURE TOPICS:

- Improving critical thinking skills
- Critical thinking errors or biases

STUDENT LEARNING OBJECTIVES:

- Investigate critical thinking and sound decision making.
- Appraise the importance of creativity and innovation in critical thinking.
- Analyze critical thinking errors and thinking traps.

A LITTLE SAMPLE OF A LECTURE DISCUSSION:

Critical thinking involves our ability to think creatively. You might need to spot patterns in the information you are reviewing or come up with a solution no one else has thought of before. All of this involves a creative eye that can take a different approach from all other approaches. The ability to conceptualize, draw connections, and synthesize are how we often describe what critical thinking entails. Good critical thinkers can draw reasonable conclusions from a set of information and discriminate between useful and less useful details to solve problems or make decisions. Critical thinking is very important in most jobs today because there is less direct supervision and there are more opportunities to access information as a normal part of work. One of the most important aspects of critical thinking is the fact that you need to be able to put aside any assumptions or judgments and merely analyze the information you receive. You need to be objective, evaluating ideas without bias. It requires you to be reflective and observant.

PROBLEM SOLVING

PUZZLE HANDOUT:

Puzzle #1:

Use the letters below to spell out just one word.

D E J N O O R S T U W

Puzzle #2:

Cross out six letters to reveal one word.

S O I N X L E T E W T O E R R D S

Puzzle #3:

A woman has the following dilemma: she needs to get a fox, a chicken, and a bag of corn across to the other side of a river in as few moves as possible. She has a rowboat, but it can only carry her and one other item at a time.

Her dilemma is clear—she cannot leave the fox and the chicken alone together (the fox will eat the chicken) and she cannot leave the chicken with the corn (the chicken will eat the corn).

To govern fair play, the solution must acknowledge three critical parameters:

- The rowboat can only carry one person and one item at any point in time.
- The fox and chicken cannot be left alone.
- The chicken and the bag of corn cannot be left alone.

Describe the step-by-step solution to get all three items safely to the other side of the river.

SOLUTIONS:

Puzzle #1: JUST ONE WORD

Puzzle #2: Cross out "SIXLETTERS" and you are left with "ONE WORD"

Puzzle #3:

To begin, the woman and the chicken cross the river together. The fox and corn are safe together.

Once on the other side, the woman leaves the chicken and returns to the fox and corn. She takes the fox across the river, and since she can't leave the fox and chicken together, she brings the chicken back with her (that's the trick that many groups do not think of).

She cannot leave the chicken with the corn, so she leaves the chicken and rows the corn across the river and leaves it with the fox.

Finally, she returns to pick up the chicken and rows across the river one last time.

Adapted from:

Scannell, M., & Cain, J. (2012). Puzzles and Games with Teachable Moments. In *Big Book of Low-Cost Training Games: Quick, Effective Activities that Encourage Out-of-the-Box Thinking, Improve Collaboration, and Spark Great Ideas!* (1st ed., p. 135). New York, NY: McGraw Hill

GAME: FRACTURED T

GAME: FRACTURED T

INTRODUCTION:

Effective communication is essential in any environment. This activity explores such challenges and encourages groups to find communication techniques that are effective and efficient.

PURPOSE/OBJECTIVE:

To foster communication and listening skills.

GROUP SIZE:

15 students (if more, adjust the number of copies and bags needed for each participant).

MATERIALS:

Timer. Five Paper bags. Ten different sheets of color copy paper.

Fractured T Handout: Fractured T.

TIME: 20–25 minutes.

PRE-GAME PROCEDURE:

1. Make copies of the Fracture T handout using five different printer paper colors. Take each Fracture T handout and cut out all five of the pieces. Keep them together. Then mix different pieces to create five Fractured Ts where each

of the five pieces is a different color. In other words, you will have a Fractured T made up of five different color pieces. Take five paper lunch bags and write **number 1** on the outside of each paper bag with a marker. Inside each bag, place a folded Fractured T handout and a set of the five color pieces that make up a T. You should be able to prepare five lunch bags.

2. Make copies of the Fracture T handout using five additional different color printer paper. Take each Fracture T handout and cut out all five of the pieces. Keep them together. Then mix different pieces to create five Fractured Ts where each of the five pieces is a different color. In other words, you will have a Fractured T made up of five different color pieces. Take five paper lunch bags and write **number 2** on the outside of each paper bag with a marker. Inside each bag, place a set of the five color pieces that make up a Fractured T. You should be able to prepare five lunch bags. ***Note: This bag does not have a copy of the Fractured T handout.***

PROCEDURE:

Divide the group into sets of three students. Tell the students each of them will be given a role. Role number 1 is a teacher, role number 2 is a learner, and role number 3 is an observer. Ask them to decide among themselves who will take which role. Then, ask the learner to leave until called back into the room.

Give lunch bag labeled number 1 to each of the students who chose to be teachers. Let everyone know that the purpose of the teacher is to have the second person put together the shape of a T *without* letting them know the overall T shape. They can look into the bag to familiarize themselves with the contents.

Let them know that they can describe each of the individual five pieces to guide the learner to achieve the overall shape of a T. The role of the observer is to do just that. They are to take notes and outline what strategies worked and which ones were not as effective. The observer cannot speak nor give directions/instructions.

Request the learners to return and stand back-to-back to their "teacher." Provide the learner with the bag labeled number 2. Let them know the teacher will be guiding them to use the pieces they have in their bag to come up with the desired overall shape. The observer stands close by to observe the interactions between the teacher and the learner. The observer will quickly realize that the teacher and the learner have different colored shapes and will be able to witness the interaction and the ability of the teacher to think creatively and "teach" in a way that the learner can understand.

Instruct all of the students to work on it independently for the next five to eight minutes. After one or two minutes, ask them how they are coming along. By this time, some of the teachers are beginning to lose their patience as they assume they both have the same color pieces. Typically, at this point in the game, the teachers begin describing each individual piece without using colors as a guide. Have some fun facilitating this session. If a team completes the project, give the other teams a few more minutes to complete the task. You can wait until all teams complete the task or stop the game and begin to debrief it.

Call observers to the front and have them share (or write on the board) their observations. Have them explain what strategies worked and which ones did not in solving the puzzle.

DISCUSSION QUESTIONS:

- What were the barriers to effective communication?
- Why did you think the colors of each of the shapes were the same for the teacher and learner?
- How did you adapt your messaging as a teacher? How did you adapt your listening?

GENERAL QUESTIONS:

- What did you learn?
- Was this experience worthwhile?

SUGGESTED LECTURE TOPICS:

- Managing communication
- Becoming a more effective communicator

STUDENT LEARNING OBJECTIVES:

- Evaluate the nature and function of communication.
- Formulate how to become a better communicator.

A LITTLE SAMPLE OF A LECTURE DISCUSSION:

For communication to be successful, the meaning must be imparted and understood. It takes the idea to be received exactly as envisioned by the sender. Communication does not mean agreement with the message; it simply means a clear understanding of the message. If a person disagrees with us or does not seem to understand our point of view, we assume the person simply does not understand. Such assumption could not be farther from the truth. It could very well mean they clearly understood your message, but just don't agree with what you say.

Another common way in which we fail to communicate is by making assumptions. During this activity, many teachers assumed the learner had the same color pieces as you. Assumptions are nothing but communication shortcuts. We rush to convey our message across when in reality, had we taken a little bit of time to ascertain a common ground, you would have been able to deliver and achieve the goal sooner. Sometimes, as professionals, we assume our patients, customers, or employees understand our words. From afar, it might seem like you are on the same page, but if you do not take the time to confirm basic assumptions, you have failed to communicate without realizing it.

Provided by:
Sara Lynn Terrell, PhD, CSCS*D, USAW-L1
Associate Professor, Exercise Science
Exercise Science Program Director
Florida Southern College

FRACTURED T HANDOUT

GAME: BALL POINT GAME

INTRODUCTION:

Understanding the importance of adaptation and agility is essential at any stage of our personal and professional lives. This activity combines adaptability and critical thinking. It challenges and encourages groups to learn and adapt quickly in order to meet expected outcomes.

PURPOSE/OBJECTIVE:

The objective of the Ball Point Game is to get as many individual plastic balls as possible through a group of students within two minutes. The objective is to exercise critical thinking, teamwork, and adaptability.

GROUP SIZE: Any.

MATERIALS:

Timer. Large open space with enough room for everyone to stand. One hundred brightly colored tennis or plastic balls (note: you should have enough balls to give twenty to thirty balls per team). A 20x23 self-stick wall Post-it notepad. Markers. Boxes for each team to collect the balls.

MUSIC: Classic rock from the '80s and '90s.

TIME: 30–35 minutes.

PROCEDURE:

1) Divide the group into sets of twelve students. The more teams you have, the more competition is created, and energy increases. Explain to the teams that they are to pass as many balls through their team as possible within four minutes. They will have five consecutive attempts to increase the output. The teams will have five minutes in between attempts to help them ideate a new solution. The rules for the movement of the balls are as follows:

1. Each ball must have airtime.
2. Each ball must be touched at least once by every team member.
3. Balls cannot be passed to the person on your immediate left or right.
4. Each ball must return to the same person who introduced it into the system.
5. Once the ball returns to the person who introduced it to the system, it can go into the "processed" box.
6. Each "processed" ball that makes it through the entire process and thus into the box counts as one point.
7. Any ball that falls to the ground results in a penalty for the team. Three points are deducted from the total "processed" count at the end of each iteration.

Variation Rule:

You can explain to the team that any ball that drops to the ground can be picked up and reintroduced into the system. If it makes it through the entire process, no points are deducted.

2) Share with students that you will provide six minutes to organize themselves and think through their strategy.

3) While the teams are organizing themselves, provide each team with a Post-it note and markers. Have each team select a member who will be responsible for annotating on the Post-it notepad the team's performance. Explain to each team that they are to write their goal on how many balls they will successfully pass through their individual system for the first round. At the end of the round, each team is to write the outcome and compare against their goal. The teams will annotate their goal and performance each round.

4) Start the first four-minute iteration. Have one member of each team verbally share their outcomes to the entire group.

5) Allow the teams five minutes to discuss how to improve the process. Repeat four more times.

VARIATION:

Right before the fifth iteration, share with students that you will provide x number of extra credit points to the members of the team that end with the highest number of balls through the system.

DISCUSSION QUESTIONS:

It is vital that you allocate at least twenty to thirty minutes for discussion/debrief immediately after the game is completed as doing so will allow students time to verbalize self-realizations leading to deeper learning. After the free time for discussions, lead with some of the following discussion questions:

- What did you learn?
- Was this experience worthwhile?
- How did you organize yourselves at first? Were there any changes in the way you organized yourselves at the end?
- How did your team make decisions?
- Did someone rise to a leadership status?
- How much did you change your process after having time to reassess?
- Why would we deduct three points for each ball dropped?

SUGGESTED LECTURE TOPICS:

- Deming cycle
- SCRUM concepts
- Defects
- Opportunity costs
- Quality versus quality
- Theory of constraints
- Lean/Six Sigma concepts
- First to market concepts
- Group formation and groupthink concepts
- Hidden costs of multitasking
- Servant leadership

STUDENT LEARNING OBJECTIVES:

- Solve or innovate a solution to the problem presented.
- Discern SCRUM concepts to the activity.

- Discern the concept of opportunity cost and its relationship to defects.
- Formulate the relationship between quality and quantity.
- Apply the theory of constraints from the activity.
- Discern Lean/Six Sigma concepts.
- Discern the importance of first to marker from the activity.
- Describe groups and the stages of group development.
- Relate the concept of multitasking to the activity.
- Relate the concept of servant leadership to the activity.

A LITTLE SAMPLE OF A LECTURE DISCUSSION:

The high cost of a dropped ball represents defects. The reason dropped balls must go through the entire process again is because defects yield expensive rework. Processes that are not corrected at first must be corrected later, and now the time spent in correcting the problem has doubled. But why deduct three points? It can be argued that the time spent correcting the problem is time that could have been spent producing more "processed" balls representing an *opportunity cost.*

In terms of working harder or smarter, this activity highlights the idea that with each iteration, the team had less physical activity and fewer defects. You do not have to work faster to improve the score. In fact, moving too fast results in lower quality or more dropped balls. The best way to work was at a quick, constant, and sustainable pace.

Additionally, it is important to note that all of you had to work together to devise a plan. This very feeling is called empowerment. As a future leader, you must resist the temptation to provide all the answers and *invest* in your team's culture.

This investment will pay itself back as your team improves and continues to innovate in unexpected and rewarding ways.

Created by:
Boris Gloger created the Ball Point Game in 2008 to teach Scrum concepts. The game is a great opportunity to introduce people to basic principles in agility.

Adapted by:
Dr. Silviana Falcon

GAME: THE CASE OF TWO BALLOONS

PURPOSE:

Highlights the importance of personal values and their relationship to ethical decision-making.

GROUP SIZE: ANY.

MATERIALS:

Two 10-inch balloons. Multipurpose utility lighter.

PRE-GAME PROCEDURE:

Fill one of the 10-inch balloons with water and keep it and the multi-purpose lighter from the student's view.

TIME: 10–15 minutes.

PROCEDURE:

Share with students, that you will cover values and ethics during your lecture, but before you do so, you want to learn a little more about them and what they value. In other words, what represents their basic convictions about what is right and what is wrong? Share with students that humanist psychologists have proposed that people have an innate sense of values and personal preferences, and that research has shown that values are learned and strengthened, or even changed, through our human journey. This is the reason why it is a good idea to become more conscious of the strength of our values or convictions because they are our best guide on how to live a better life.

Tell students that you want them to pretend they are the balloon you hold in your hand. Ask them to share with you what they currently value. As students share a value, acknowledge it and then blow air into the balloon as if the balloon acquired such value. As students provide more examples of values they hold dear, keep inflating the balloon until it is fully inflated. Make a knot and hold it up for them to be able to see it.

Now, share with students an ethical dilemma. Tell them that this person (represented by the balloon) was the last person in the classroom last week. She noticed the professor left behind a folder labeled final exam. Instinctively, she opens the folder and, indeed, there is a copy of the class' final exam. What should she do? What values (from the values identified) could help her guide her decision? (This question typically yields a lot of discussion among students.) As students debate her next action, bring out the multipurpose lighter and apply some heat to the bottom of the balloon, making sure you move the heat source quickly past the balloon (so that it will not pop).

After some discussion, I share that the student decided to return the exam to the professor. On her way to her office, she encounters a couple of friends. She shares with them the whole story and her friends ask her to take pictures of the exam so they can sell it. Again, invite students to share their thoughts and debate among themselves what the course of action for the student who found the exam should be. At this point, ask students who do not like loud noises to please cover their ears. Then, place the lighter closer to the balloon, which will explode rather quickly because the rubber of the balloon becomes so hot that it becomes too weak to resist the pressure of the air inside the balloon. This is a perfect analogy to show that any person can break to temptation or external pressures if the strength of their convictions is not strong enough (possess a low ego strength and an external locus of control).

Next, I bring out the balloon previously filled with water. Share with students that this is the same person as before with the same outlined values. This person also feels strong external pressure from her friends. At this point, use the utility lighter and apply heat to the balloon (it will not burst). The students are typically amazed at the fact that the balloon is not bursting. For effect, just keep applying heat to the balloon; it will not burst, as the water will absorb most of the heat from the flame. Because the rubber does not become hot, it does not weaken and, consequently, the balloon does not break. When the water gets hot enough, the balloon will break from within. This is a great analogy to show that a person's strength in their convictions will help maneuver through our life's journey, which is riddled with ethical dilemmas. Nothing is foolproof, but having strong convictions certainly influences a person to behave ethically and be more likely to encourage ethical behavior in others.

After this activity, students are primed to learn more about ethics, law and ethics, stages of moral development, and issue intensity. No additional discussion questions are necessary.

However, consider using a one-minute paper at the end of the class lecture to have students think through their learning and share with you, the professor, their additional thoughts. You will be amazed at the reasoning this simple activity yields.

SUGGESTED LECTURE TOPICS:

- Factors determining ethical and unethical behavior
- Kohlberg's stages of moral development
- Ego strength and locus of control
- Code of ethics

STUDENT LEARNING OBJECTIVES:

- Appraise the factors that lead to ethical and unethical behaviors.
- Analyze and evaluate Kohlberg's stages of moral development.
- Differentiate between ego strength and locus of control.
- Infer the importance of a code of ethics.

Adapted from:

CHEMICAL DEMONSTRATIONS: A Handbook for Teachers of Chemistry, Volume 3, by Bassam Z. Shakhashiri, The University of Wisconsin Press, 2537 Daniels Street, Madison, Wisconsin 53704.

FOCUSED:

ACCENTUATING STRENGTHS; MINIMIZING WEAKNESSES

EFFECTIVE DECISION MAKING

PROCEDURES MATTER

AS THE COOKIE CRUMBLES

TURNING DATA INTO INFORMATION

EFFICIENCY AND EFFECTIVENESS

CULTURAL DIFFERENCES

INTERNATIONAL TRADING GAME

STARPOWER

ACCENTUATING STRENGTHS, MINIMIZING WEAKNESSES

GAME: SANTA CLAUSE SWOT ANALYSIS

INTRODUCTION:

This is a simple game to help students understand **SWOT** analysis as a critical and often used tool used to identify a person's or a company's strengths, weaknesses, opportunities, and threats. The primary objective of a SWOT analysis is to develop a full awareness of internal and external factors involved in making a personal or business decision.

This game allows the students to adapt a concept from their childhood and apply it by learning a new strategic tool. The goal is not only to determine what is written on each quadrant, but also to develop a strategy or course of action capitalizing on strengths and opportunities, all while minimizing the weaknesses and threats.

VARIATIONS:

Each team can select a superhero. This tool can also be used to have students conduct a SWOT analysis of their own professional lives to develop a strategy for their future success.

PURPOSE/OBJECTIVES:

SWOT is a strategic development tool that matches internal organizational **S**trengths (positive characteristics) and

Weaknesses (negative characteristics) with external **O**pportunities (what are others doing that I could do) and **T**hreats (what is happening that can have a negative impact). The main purpose of conducting a SWOT analysis is to provide a well-researched foundation upon which to formulate a plan or strategy to move the organization forward. Through this game, students learn to brainstorm, collect ideas, and critically think beyond the four squares to transform them into a plan of action.

GROUP SIZE: Any.

MATERIALS: SWOT Analysis Handout.

TIME: 30–40 minutes.

PROCEDURE:

Break out students into teams of four. Complete a **SWOT** Analysis on Santa Clause, listing his/her strengths, weaknesses, opportunities, and threats.

After the students complete the SWOT analysis, they must develop two to three strategies focused on highlighting the strengths, minimizing the identified threats, and seizing the outlined opportunities. The strategies should answer, at minimum, how they will you use the strengths to take advantage of stated opportunities, how will they combat weaknesses, and how will they address threats to Santa Clause.

Students are then to select a member of their team to share one of the most significant strategies they formulated. This is an opportunity to help all students learn from one another as they can experience how the SWOT analysis tool can yield a plan of action.

MUSIC:

Playing Santa Clause- or Superhero-themed music allows students to relax and have fun.

DISCUSSION QUESTIONS:

- How does this activity relate to how we conduct a SWOT for an organization?
- Was the information helpful in developing the strategies?
- What could be some of the drawbacks of the SWOT analysis tool?

GENERAL QUESTIONS:

- What did you learn?
- Was this experience worthwhile?

SUGGESTED LECTURE TOPICS:

- Planning for the future
- What is strategy
- Planning for uncertainty

STUDENT LEARNING OBJECTIVES:

- Evaluate and analyze the importance of strategy.
- Analyze the strategic planning process.
- Construct and appraise a SWOT analysis.
- Implement the use of a SWOT analysis to your own life.

A LITTLE SAMPLE OF A LECTURE DISCUSSION:

A carefully orchestrated SWOT analysis allows you to create a plan that will actually work since it helps prioritize areas that need to be enhanced, and areas that need to be eliminated. This process allows a company (or yourself) to maximize its opportunities, anticipate and overcome threats to its survival, and do it all in a timely and cost-efficient manner.

SWOT TEMPLATE:

SWOT Analysis Template

*State what you are assessing here*____________________

(This particular example is for a new business opportunity. Many criteria can apply to more than one quadrant. Identify criteria appropriate too your own SWOT situation.)

Criteria examples	Strengths	Weaknesses	Criteria examples
Advantages of proposition Capabilities Competitive advantages USP's (unique selling points) Resources, Assets, People Experience, knowledge, data Financial reserves, likely returns Marketing - reach, distribution, awareness Innovative aspects Location and geographical Price, value, quality Accreditations, qualifications, certifications Processes, systems, IT, communications			Disadvantages of proposition Gaps in capabilities Lack of competitive strength Reputation, presence and reach Financials Own known vulnerabilities Timescales, deadlines and pressures Cash flow, start-up cash-drain Continuity, supply chain robustness Effects on core activities, distruction Reliability of data, plan predictability Morale, commitment, leadership Accreditations etc
Criteria examples	**Opportunities**	**Threats**	**Criteria examples**
Market developments Competitors' vulnerabilities Industry or lifestyle trends Technology development and innovation Global influences New markets, vertical, horizontal Niche target markets Geographical, export, import New USP's Tactics: eg, surprise, major contacts Business and product development Information and research Partnerships, agencies			Political effects Legislative effects Environmental effects IT developments Competitor intentions - various Market demand New technologies, services, ideas Vital contracts and partners Sustaining internal capabilities Obstacles faced Insurmountable weaknesses Loss of key staff Sustainable financial backing Economy - home, abroad Seasonality, weather effects

Source:

Pacific Crest Group. SWOT Analysis-Get Going on Growth!. Accessed November 12, 2020. https://www.pcg-services.com/swot-analysis-growth/

Example of completed Santa Clause SWOT analysis.

Strengths	Weaknesses
Loyal Customers High level of Awareness Strong Brand Image – Ho..Ho..Ho.. Catch Phrase Omnipotent – maybe even magic Keeps overheads to a minimum Kids really like Santa Kids write to him – knows exactly what they need	Santa is a control freak – may not have the best management style Morbidly obese at 35 stone – fitness for work? No investment in infrastructure Delivers the entire stock on only 1 sled – risk of mechanical problems Evidence that Santa is an alcoholic – drinks 15,000 gallons of sherry and whisky in one night
Opportunities	**Threats**
Growing world population To deliver to ALL kids – not just the ones that have been good Diversify – use a talking meerkat (or similar) to attract a new customer base Deliver the toys 2 days earlier – for a premium gold card subscription. Pimp my Sleigh Social media presence	Internet sales – all year round RSPCA may inspect – but no evidence of animal cruelty House building – chimneys getting smaller Might get caught drinking on the job Lack of belief in modern teenagers – easy access to information Flatulence – methane emissions from old reindeer

Source:
Consultants Online. SWOT Analysis Santa's Grotto. Accessed November 12, 2020

http://www.consultants-on-line.com/default.asp?contentID=144

GAME: EFFECTIVE DECISION-MAKING

INTRODUCTION:

Our personal and professional lives require us to constantly make decisions—from minor to significant and everything in between. Good decision-making is a skill and, as such, it can be learned and improved. This game allows students to use a personal life situation and applying what they know in order to learn the eight-step decision-making process. A summary of the distinct steps is as follows:

Step 1: Identifying a problem or what needs to be decided: This is the most important STEP of all. We must make the distinction between the current situation and the desired situation.

Step 2: Establish the decision criteria: Identify or determine the guiding criteria. In other words, what is most important or relevant to solving the identified problem?

Step 3: Weighting the criteria: Not all criteria will have the same importance when it comes to making the final decision. Thus, we must prioritize the criteria selected in the previous step.

Step 4: Considering the options or alternatives: Identify all the feasible options that might successfully resolve the problem.

Step 5: Analyze the option or alternatives: This is the evaluative section of the decision-making process. It requires the decision maker to study the proposed options in detail. The strengths and weaknesses of each one should become clear when compared against the selected criteria.

Step 6: Selecting an alternative: This is the moment of truth. Just one option must be selected; the best of the options is selected.

Step 7: Implementing the alternative option: Once the selection is process over, the implementation of the chosen alternative becomes vitally important.

Step 8: Assessing the effectiveness of the decision: Finally, we must assess if the problem has been corrected. If, however, the problem persists, the process will have to be reviewed to identify any mistakes along the way.

PURPOSE/OBJECTIVE:

Decision-making is a process, not just a simple act of choosing among alternatives. The objective is to help students understand there is a method to making decisions that involves identifying the problem to evaluating the effectiveness of that decision. While this model has limitations, it serves to rationally identify a problem and choose and implement an alternative.

GROUP SIZE: Any.

MATERIALS: Decision-Making Handout (Who to Date).

TIME: 30–40 minutes.

PROCEDURE:

Provide the decision-making handout to each participant. Tell the students that the problem they face is that they would like to go out on a date with someone special. However, so it happens that they have been invited by three different individuals. So, how will they decide among the three individuals?

Provide the students time to decipher the problem and the criteria. As a facilitator, ask a couple of the students to share their description of the problem and their chosen criteria. Provide feedback so the entire group can learn or offer other potential criteria (e.g., sense of humor, positive attitude, etc.). See the example provided below.

In terms of alternatives, have them choose a famous personality, such as Brad Pitt, Angelina Jolie, Drake, etc. to make it a fun activity.

Allow another ten to fifteen minutes for students to complete the entire form and determine the selected alternative. Ask a few of the students to discuss their alternatives and result.

DISCUSSION QUESTIONS:

- Is there a difference between wrong decisions and bad decisions?
- Why do we make wrong decisions? Bad decisions?
- How can you use data to improve decision-making?

General Questions:

- What did you learn?
- Was this experience worthwhile?

Suggested Lecture Topics:

- Decision-making process
- What is strategy
- Planning for uncertainty

STUDENT LEARNING OBJECTIVES:

Construct, appraise , and analyze a decision following the eight steps in the decision-making process.

A LITTLE SAMPLE OF A LECTURE DISCUSSION:

Decision-making is at the heart of everything we do (or even try to avoid). We all try to make the best decisions each day—especially at work, as our performance is evaluated based on the outcomes of those decisions. Effective and successful decisions yield a profit to the company and unsuccessful ones yield losses. Therefore, a corporate's decision-making process is critical to the overall growth and success of a company. In the process of decision-making, we may use many tools, techniques, and perceptions.

Usually, decision-making is hard. The majority of corporate decisions involve some level of dissatisfaction or conflict with another party. Let us have a look at the decision-making process in detail.

DECISION-MAKING EXAMPLE: (A CLEAN TEMPLATE OF THE FORM BELOW IS ATTACHED)

EXAMPLE FROM DECISION-MAKING SCENARIO: WHO TO DATE

SITUATION:

You have been invited by three individuals to a romantic Valentine's Day dinner. You have known all three individuals for some time and like all three of them. However, you have to select one of them, which will signal that you do want a more formal, long-term relationship. Who will you decide to go with?

STEP 1: IDENTIFY THE PROBLEM

PROBLEM: Selecting the right individual

STEP 2: IDENTIFY THE CRITERIA

STEP 3: ALLOCATE WEIGHTS TO THE CRITERIA

(1 = least important, 10 = extremely important)

CRITERIA	WEIGHT	REASONING
1 *Physical Appearance*	8	*Very attractive to you*
2 *Sense of humor*	9	*Lighthearted and funny*
3 *Supportive and respectful*	10	*Always has your back*
4 *Good listener*	9	*Listens and advises*
5 *White teeth*	7	*Important to have a bright smile*

STEP 4: DEVELOP ALTERNATIVES & ALLOCATE WEIGHTS TO EACH CRITERIA BASED ON THE INDIVIDUAL ALTERNATIVE

(For example, individual #1 is not very attractive, does not have a very strong sense of humor, and is not a good listener but is very respectful and very white teeth)

Analysis of Alternatives	1. Physical Appearance	2. Sense of Humor	3. Supportive & Respectful	4. Good listener	5. White Teeth
Individual #1	8	7	9	6	10
Individual #2	10	5	8	7	4
Individual #3	7	6	10	10	9

STEP 5: ANALYZE ALTERNATIVES

(Multiply the weight given to each criteria and the weights given to each individual based on the criteria). Add all of the scores. Select the individual with the highest score.

Analysis of Alternatives	1. Physical Appearance	2.Sense of Humor	3. Supportive & Respectful	4. Good listener	5. White Teeth	TOTAL
Individual #1	8 x 8 = **64**	9 x 7 = **63**	10 x 9 = **90**	9 x 6 = **54**	7x10 = **70**	341
Individual #2	8 x 10 = **80**	9 x 5 = **45**	10 x 8 = **80**	9 x 7 = **63**	7x 7 = **49**	317
Individual #3	8 x 7 = **56**	9 x 6 = **54**	10x10 = **100**	9x10 = **90**	7x9 = **63**	363

STEP 6: SELECT THE ALTERNATIVE: Individual #3

STEP 7: IMPLEMENT THE ALTERNATIVE:

Accept Individual #3's invitation to dinner.

STEP 8: EVALUATE THE EFFECTIVENESS OF THE ALTERNATIVE:

Was it the right choice? Anything you would have changed regarding the decision criteria?

DECISION-MAKING SCENARIO HANDOUT

STEP 1: (Problem)

STEP 2 & 3: Decision Criteria and Allocate Weight (i.e., prioritize)

Decision Criteria	Allocate Weights
1.	
2.	
3.	
4.	

STEP 4: Develop Alternatives

Alternatives	Decision Criteria 1: ______	Decision Criteria 2: ______	Decision Criteria 3: ______	Decision Criteria 4: ______

STEP 5: ANALYZE THE ALTERNATIVES

Alternatives	Decision Criteria 1: ______	Decision Criteria 2: ______	Decision Criteria 3: ______	Decision Criteria 4: ______	Total

STEP 6: SELECT THE ALTERNATIVE:

____

STEP 7: IMPLEMENT THE ALTERNATIVE:

____

STEP 8: EVALUATE THE EFFECTIVENESS OF THE ALTERNATIVE:

____

GAME: PROCEDURES MATTER

INTRODUCTION:

Giving clear, concise, replicable instructions to others is an important professional soft skill to acquire.

PURPOSE/OBJECTIVE:

Students are able to recognize importance of taking time to create clear procedures for others to follow.

GROUP SIZE: Any.

MATERIALS:

Two jars of peanut (or almond) butter, two jellies in a squeezable bottle, one (or more) bags of bread, two butter knives, two plates, gloves for the volunteers, two rolls of paper towels, a large trash bag (I usually have enough materials to make a PB&J sandwich for each student to eat after class).

PRE-WORK:

Safety considerations: Some students may have peanut allergies. As you plan to play this activity, make sure you ask ahead of the lecture and activity if any of your students are allergic to peanut butter. I send out a notification via email so that students can respond only to me via email to keep their information restricted. If allergies are identified, you can use bagels and cream cheese or something similar.

Have two tables set up in the front so the students can see each of the volunteers working on making the sandwiches. Both tables are set up exactly in the same fashion with all items set out except for the jelly, which is kept from view. **Note:** students will assume the jelly will come in a jar and not on a squeezable bottle. Thus, you can discuss how our own bias lead to confusion.

TIME: 50–60 minutes.

MUSIC:

Jeopardy song or something fun to help students think.

PROCEDURE:

Share with all students that the objective of the activity is to successfully outline a procedure so that any one person can make a peanut (or almond) butter and jelly sandwich. Let them know that they are to use their experience making a peanut butter and jelly sandwich in teaching someone else how to successfully make a sandwich. Share with students that details matter.

Ask for a couple of volunteers who will be responsible for listening and implementing the procedure and thus ultimately and successfully making peanut (or almond) butter and jelly sandwiches for the entire class.

Step 1: Have students work individually and write an outline procedure. Allow them between five to eight minutes to work on their own.

As students are working individually, have the volunteers sit at the table. They can put on their gloves and arrange their workstations. Share with the volunteers that, you will call on a set of students to give the first volunteer instructions on how to prepare the PB&J sandwich. The first volunteer must follow the instructions exactly and stop making the sandwich at the point the instructions are not clear or wrong pointing out what went wrong. The first volunteer proceeds to clean up the space as the facilitator calls on a second set of students. The second volunteer works on following the instructions exactly and stops making the sandwich at the point where the instructions are not clear or wrong pointing out what went wrong. The second volunteer cleans up the space and gets ready for another round. The facilitator keeps calling on groups of students until the instructions are so clear that one of the volunteers is successful at making a PB&J sandwich.

Step 2: Have students work with the person next to them and compare their procedures. Have them make changes and update their own procedure now that they learned and compared notes with someone else. Allow five minutes for students to work in pairs.

Step 3: Have students now share their work with a second set of students. In essence, four students will be working together, comparing notes, adjusting and improving their procedure. Allow five minutes for students to work in groups of four.

Step 4: Share with all students that you will call on a set of students. They will read the instructions on how to make the PB&J sandwich to the first volunteer who will follow the instructions as given. At any point where the instructions are wrong or not accurate, the volunteer will stop making the sandwich. You will then call on another set of students to give the second volunteer their set of instructions. It is important to share with students that they must be attentive to what is happening and adjust their instructions as the activity takes place, improving their narrative each time and noting where they missed steps or went wrong.

The first group of students' instructions will be found to be wrong soon into the sandwich-making process because most of the students write their procedure with the assumption that the jelly will come in a jar instead of a squeezable bottle. As the second and third group of students are called, their instructions keep perfecting until the PB&J sandwich is finally produced. By this time, students are very energized and looking forward to enjoying their sandwich.

Discussion Questions:

- What assumptions did you make that proved to be correct?
- What did you miss and why?
- How would you minimize procedural errors?

ENERAL QUESTIONS:

- What did you learn?
- Was this experience worthwhile?

SUGGESTED LECTURE TOPICS:

- The impact of bias
- The importance of replicability in scientific studies
- The difference between policies and procedures

STUDENT LEARNING OBJECTIVES:

- Formulate/author a standard operating procedure.
- Evaluate the impact and importance of following a procedure.
- Analyze the steps necessary for writing a procedure.

A LITTLE SAMPLE OF A LECTURE DISCUSSION:

Procedures are the railroad tracks that get people from point A to point B consistently and without error. Procedures are the way to show the "how to" get there. Procedures are action oriented. They outline steps to take and the order in which they need to be taken. Well written procedures are typically solid, precise, factual, short, and to the point. Take research as an example—outlining a procedure is vital in successfully recreating the conditions of, and reproducing the original experiment, which is at the cornerstone of sharing empirically gained knowledge.

Provided by:
Sara Lynn Terrell, PhD, CSCS*D, USAW-L1
Associate Professor, Exercise Science
Exercise Science Program Director

Adapted by:
Dr. Silviana Falcon
Florida Southern College

GAME: AS THE COOKIE CRUMBLES

PURPOSE/OBJECTIVE:

This exercise can be positioned to either kick off a learning unit on Porter's five forces model or to end a unit by creating an experience that makes an academic model come alive.

GROUP SIZE: 12–50

MATERIALS:

Cookies (the larger the better). Knives/plates/gloves/hand sanitizer. Icing/sprinkles/decorating gels/candy. Hats for each of Porter's roles: supplier, buyer, new company, existing, and new technology.

TIME: 45–60 minutes.

PRE-GAME PROCEDURE:

Flexible rooms with movable tables are optimal.

Set up industry zones of twelve students or as many zones as needed.

Room Setup Guidelines: Cookie Crumbles handout.

Choose student observers ahead of time to help set up.

Hats for each role of the exercise should be placed on each student's seat.

Mix up students from usual groups to increase dynamics.

PROCEDURE:

The premise of the exercise is that each zone represents an active industry cell. The industry is "decorated cookies" as one might find in department stores. Cookies are used to brand special occasions, seasons, sports teams, or other elaborate designs. The "buyers" in the industry are defined as two separate department store corporations. Typically, one is considered a mid-price chain such as Kohl's or JCPenney, and the other is a higher-end chain such as Saks Fifth Ave or Bonwit Teller.

The goal is for companies to create prototypes of decorated cookies and go into a contractual relationship with one of the buyers.

The classroom is set up to mirror Porter's five forces by rearranging tables and placing a "role hat" on each chair (see Figure 2). One model of this exercise can accommodate the following number of students: new market entrants (2), suppliers (2), buyers (2), disruptive substitutes (2) and existing company (4), for a total of twelve roles. By having two students operate in a similar Porter role (e.g., buyer, supplier, disrupter), competition or the opportunity for collaboration increases, which also increases engagement. The introduction of different buyers allows students the opportunity to explore how consumer needs may vary based on the niche they exist within. All of the roles are instructed to act as independent entities with the exception of the existing company team, which is positioned in the middle of the zone, facing each other at the same table. As an existing company, they have the advantage of more resources.

In this exercise, modifications are limitless and can result in unpredictable dynamics. Thus, as the instructor, it is helpful to repeatedly pause the exercise for reflection and teaching. It is also helpful to have some students be observers so that the room includes individuals to point out topics for learning and reflection. To equalize the competition, financial success is measured by calculating the cost of one cookie prototype. For example, when companies buy from suppliers or disruptors, they have to figure out what the equivalent cost of that ingredient would be for one cookie. When companies sell prototypes to buyers (department chains), they have to specify how much the prototype costs. Buyers are evaluated on how much profit margin they would make selling what they brought. At various points in the exercise, a pause can allow for an assessment of how profitable various roles have become. This is an excellent example of doing competitive analysis and it typically results in a change of behavior.

Note:

If the class is larger, a duplicate zone can be created and positioned as existing in another geographical area. By expanding the model geographically, teachable moments can occur in how it might cost more to travel between geographies and/or customer expectations may be different. Thus, within one classroom, you can have East Coast/West Coast operations, and the exercise could even be spread across different rooms. There is also a competitive tension set up from the beginning of the exercise because there are three companies (one existing company and two start-ups) and only two buyers. Rules such as making a deal with only one company can be flexible depending on the level of competition or collaboration desired.

Next, actual cookies and decorating supplies are distributed in the exercise. Suppliers start out with some configuration of icing, cookies, knives, and candies. Disruptive substitutes are given, including squeeze nozzles and other specialty items. Existing companies start with basic supplies, and start-up companies only have a cookie, or icing, or a knife. The difficulty of the exercise is easily managed by varying the distribution of actual supplies and setting up the scenario.

RUNNING THE EXERCISE

During the exercise, several real-life scenarios play out. Existing companies tend to have some advantage based on how materials are distributed. Additionally, it is not rare to see existing companies becoming complacent and not assessing their competitive environment. Often students will remain in place and not venture to learn about the environment or what the customer wants. This is an example when the exercise can be paused for reflection or teachable moments can be made. As students begin to understand that success can come from long-term partnerships or alliances, various dynamics begin to occur.

Typically, vertical integration occurs when either an existing or start up cookie company merges with a supplier or disruptor. Sometimes supplier companies merge, and a new cookie company is born and tends to be very competitive. For the suppliers and disruptive substitute roles, profitability remains their goals too, which often leads to learning about the differences of establishing long-term supplier relationships instead of making simple transactions. This aspect of the exercise can be modified to include more of an emphasis on supply chain dynamics.

SUGGESTED LECTURE TOPICS:

- Porter's five forces model
- Elements of strategic actions
- Business disruption and innovation
- Competition
- Elements in business/financial success

- Vertical and horizontal integration
- Profit margins and competitive analysis
- Negotiation and deal making
- Mergers and acquisitions
- Strategic alliances

STUDENT LEARNING OBJECTIVES:

- Students will understand the major elements of Porter's five forces model for competitive strategy and how they may interact within an industry sector.
- Students will experience elements of strategic actions including differentiation, cost leadership, mergers, vertical integration, strategic alliances, challenges facing new industry entrants, and potential challenges facing existing companies in an industry.
- Students will gain insight in how they may interact in a business situation including, but not limited to, risk orientation, relationship building, assertiveness, sales, and deal making.

Developed by and published with expressed consent from:
Dr. Sue McNamara
Associate Professor of Management | SUNY Fredonia
References:
Kolb, D. Experiential Learning as the Science of Learning and Development. Englewood Cliffs, NJ: Prentice Hall. 1984.
Porter, M. Competitive Strategy. The Free Press/Macmillan: New York, 1980
Porter, M., "The Five Competitive Forces that Shape Strategy", Harvard Business Review, Special Issue on HB Centennial, 86, 2008.

Developed by and published with expressed consent from:
Dr. Sue McNamara
Associate Professor of Management | SUNY Fredonia

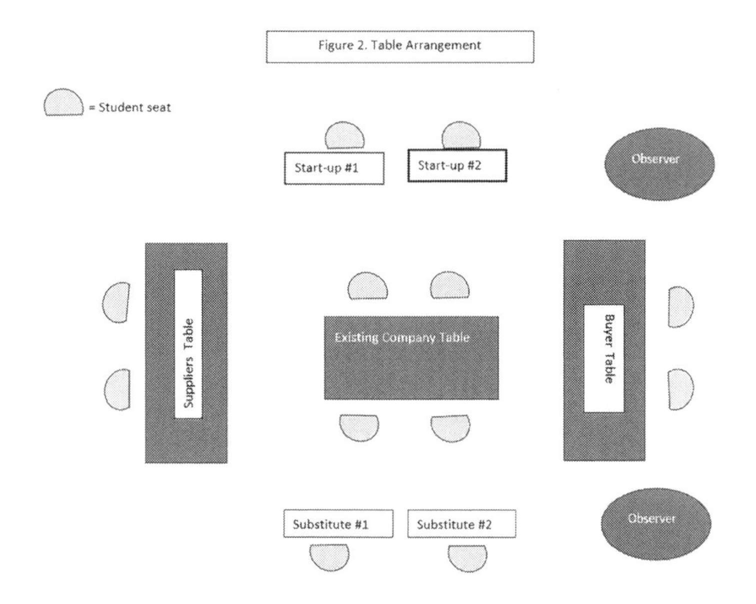

GAME: TURNING DATA INTO INFORMATION

PURPOSE/OBJECTIVES:

1) Understand the generation and collection of data and plotting on a line graph.
2) Understand upper and lower control limits.
3) Understand the importance of benchmarking.

GROUP SIZE: Any.

MATERIALS: 12 plastic cups for each team. Graph paper. Ruler. Pencil. Timer.

TIME: 50–60 minutes.

PROCEDURE:

1. Start by randomly assigning students into groups of seven.
2. Once students are in groups of seven, ask them to select one team member to be the observer who will gather data generated by the team. While the teams select the observer, provide each team with twelve plastic solo cups. Provide the observer with the graph paper, ruler, and pencil.

3. Tell all of the teams that they will stack and unstack the cups using a prearranged format of three pyramids as shown below. They must be standing around the solo cups to stack and unstack the cups.

Solo Cup Educational Activity
Pyramid Stack Example

4. Share with the teams that the goal of each team is to complete the task in the shortest amount of time.

Sequence for stacking and unstacking **all three** solo cups pyramids:

1. The first person stacks then moves away from the cups.
2. The second person unstacks and moves away from the cups.
3. The third person stacks then moves away from the cups.
4. The fourth person unstacks and moves away from the cups.
5. The fifth person stacks then moves away from the cups.
6. The sixth person unstacks and places hands on the table.
7. The observer stops the clock when the sixth participant puts both hands on the table.

8. Inform all students that unstacking can only start only after the stacker has completed the three pyramids and moves away from the table.

9. To begin, the first person places both hands on the table and, on the facilitator's instruction to "Go," begins stacking. To create a fun atmosphere, allow a couple of minutes for students to practice the task as a team before the trials begin. Play "Red Solo Cup (clean version)" by Toby Keith to liven up the room. Share with the teams that, they will conduct the entire task five times.

10. After the first trial, ask each observer to share their team's time. Write each team's time on the board or easel pad making sure it is visible to all teams. Add all of the times and divide by the number of teams to come up with the average time. This average time will be the objective (or standard) for all groups. Instruct the observer to begin a control chart denoting the team's performance time each trial and the decided-upon standard.

11. Conduct the second trial. Write each of the team's performance time on the board or easel pad, making sure it is visible to all teams. Celebrate teams that completed the second trial in less time than the first trial. Ask them to share what they changed to reduce their performance time to meet/exceed the standard. Repeat this process for trials three, four, and five. An example of how the chart should look like is provided below.

12. Determine the team with the best time. Conduct another trial only for that team and have all other teams watch them perform so they can understand from the best practice.

13. After the best team completes one trial, ask the teams what they learned from the best practice team. Allow

the teams time to voice their reasoning. What can they change/improve by adopting time-reducing techniques from the best practice team? In this last step, students often point out that the quality of work from the fastest team is compromised. This is a great example of helping students understand how an improvement in performance in one area can have a detrimental effect on another area.

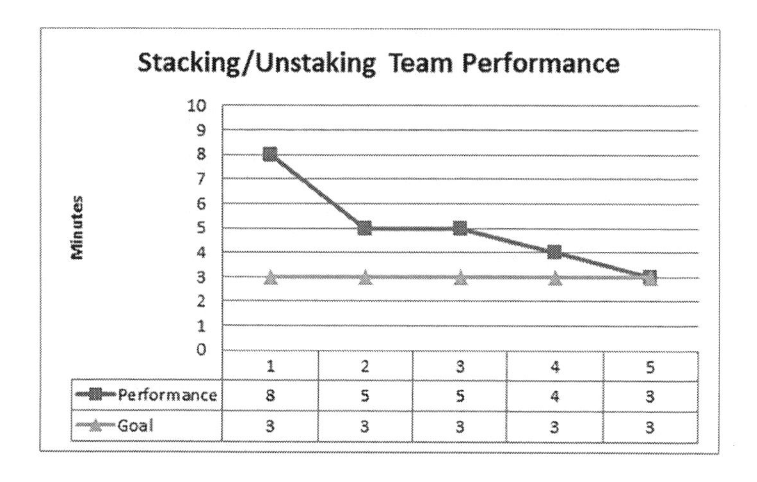

	1	2	3	4	5
Performance	8	5	5	4	3
Goal	3	3	3	3	3

DISCUSSION QUESTIONS:

- How does this game remind you of the three steps in the control process?
- We were measuring the team's performance—should we have measured each team member's performance?
- What were some immediate and basic corrective actions your team took to increase performance?
- Did we do any benchmarking? If so, when?

SUGGESTED LECTURE TOPICS:

- The control process: measuring actual performance, comparing against a standard, and taking action

- Tools for measuring organizational performance
- Strategy development
- Teamwork and performance
- Benchmarking

STUDENT LEARNING OBJECTIVES:

- Evaluate and analyze the importance of monitoring and controlling in management.
- Evaluate how to turn data into understanding and understanding into action.
- Appraise the importance of timely feedback to individual and organizational performance.
- Formulate and construct control charts as a tool to measure organizational performance.
- Appraise the importance of benchmarking and goal setting.
- Appraise process variation.

A LITTLE SAMPLE OF A LECTURE DISCUSSION:

Managers are under constant pressure to improve profitability, prompting them to uncover insights that can enhance decision making and create value. The control process establishes standards that allows us to measure and compare our performance against those standards and take corrective action(s) as necessary. As managers, we need to understand that no matter how well a process is designed, there will always be variation within the process. The variation can have a negative effect on the outcomes. This is why the controlling step in management is critically important. This phase allows managers to identify specific performance gaps and locate areas for improvement. Asking the right questions and transforming requisite data offers a new way to identify potential opportunities and make strategic changes. It allows organizations to go beyond the spreadsheet and identify what may not have been seen otherwise.

Adapted from:
Scannell, M., & Cain, J. (2009). Motivation. How Do We Stack Up?. In *Big Book of Team Motivating Games: Spirit Building, Problem Solving, and Communication Games for Every Group* (p. 59). New York, NY: McGraw Hill

GAME: EFFICIENCY AND EFFECTIVENESS

PURPOSE:.

Highlights the importance of ensuring an effective and efficient work environment as well as supporting teamwork.

GROUP SIZE: Up to 40 participants.

MATERIALS: Flip chart. Markers. Efficiency and Effectiveness Handout.

PRE-GAME PROCEDURE:

Make copies of each of the handouts, fold each handout in half, and staple at the top to prevent students from unfolding before the activity. Write the handout number with a maker clearly visible for students. Note for facilitator: The handouts are deliberately formatted in such a way to make the task difficult. For example, the numbers are not written using the same type of font ,nor the same size, nor the same direction.

TIME: 20–30 minutes.

PROCEDURE:

1. Give each student one of each of the four handouts. Have them place the handouts in order from 1 to 4. Ask them not to open any of the handouts until advised to do so.

2. Explain that the handouts represent a workplace that has gone through an iterative process of change and adaptation. Explain to students that in this activity, you, as the facilitator, are the leader (or manager) and they, as student participants, are the employees. Share with students that three prior managers were fired for their inability to bring about expected results.

3. The student's task is to strike out numbers 1 to 50 in sequential order. In other words, participants must start with finding the number 1, strike it and then move on to number 2, strike it, move on to number 3, strike it, and so on, with the goal of reaching number 50 during a single shift (sixty seconds).

Round 1: Use Handout number 1.

4. Have the students start handout number 1. Set the timer for sixty seconds and have the students begin the task. Time sixty seconds. Call stop.

5. After the first shift ends, have all students raise their hands and keep them raised as you call the numbers in sequential order, starting with number 1. Students are to lower their hand once their highest score has been called. Record on a flip chart or board the lowest score and the highest score. Have fun in this step. Create a sense of community by sharing that you do not want to be the next manager who will be fired, as you believe in their skills and capabilities.

6. After recording the highest and lowest score, ask students what they think the collective score should be. After some discussion, explain to the students that your collective

score is the lowest score because as a team, you are only as strong as the team's weakest link.

7. Explain that it is okay to have a weaker team member. Not everyone can be at the same level of skill. However, as a manager, you know there is talent among the team. At this point, request the participant who achieved the highest number sit close to the participant with the lowest number (this process is done only once). They are to work together and help each other succeed.

8. Explain to the students that in management, the number one enemy is waste. Therefore, after work, you as the facilitator convened a task force and determined that since our task is to strike out numbers 1 to 50, there is no reason to have numbers 61 to 90 in our workspace (handout). Explain that the task force conducted a time study and identified 61 to 90 are part of old processes "of the way we used to do things around here" and, therefore, are no longer valid so they can be taken out. Next, explain to students that the chief executive officer is willing to provide the team and my leadership a second opportunity given the time studies and strategic operational changes made.

Round 2: Use Handout number 2.

9. Using the handout labeled as number 2, repeat the task of striking out numbers 1 to 50 in sequential order during a single shift (60 seconds). Typically, significant improvement is made. Record on the board the lowest score and the highest score. The lowest score becomes the team's score. By now, the team is energized. The lowest score typically doubles by now.

Round 3: Use Handout Number 3.

10. Explain that as a manager, you have installed a grid system to better organize the work. The numbers are viewed more effectively as they are in smaller, more organized groups. Since the new system created expenditures, the CEO has agreed to continue to provide another opportunity to the team so long as continued improvement is achieved... with the caveat that the work is completed more efficiently (Rather than a sixty-second shift, change to a fifty-second shift). Use handout labeled number 3, set the timer, and repeat the task for fifty seconds. Record the lowest and highest score. At this time, students are energized, as some are able to strike up to fifty numbers.

Round 4: Use Handout number 4.

11. Explain that as a manager, you have negotiated an incentive program that will pay a bonus to each employee if the goal of achieving all 50 numbers in sequential order is met within the shift consistently. By now, the participant's level of energy is high. Explain that you have further improved the workplace by enhancing the grid system where every number has a place. Use handout labeled number 4, set the timer, and repeat the task using the fifty-second shift. At this time, students are energized, as all are able to strike up to sixty numbers, which is well beyond expectations. However, they quickly realize that number 51 is missing. This number has been missing since the beginning of the activity.

DISCUSSION QUESTIONS:

Since the game creates a lot of energy, it is important to allow time for the students to share their learning as open discussion **before** you start asking pointed questions.

Here are additional questions you can ask:

- What did you find the most challenging about this game?
- Did you see any evidence of teamwork, organization, motivation?
- What did you think about incentivizing work performance?
- What did you think about the process? Did you see any of the 5s Lean Concepts?

SUGGESTED LECTURE TOPICS:

- Managing and leading teams
- Productivity
- Variation
- Problem identification
- Teamwork
- Building team skills
- 5s Lean Concepts

STUDENT LEARNING OBJECTIVES:

- Evaluate and analyze the power of teamwork and best practices for influencing group performance.
- Evaluate the importance of time studies.
- Evaluate and analyze 5s Lean Concepts.

A LITTLE SAMPLE OF A LECTURE DISCUSSION:

The more time we spend understanding a problem and involving the people who are at the front line of the problem, the more effective the resolution will be. Great managers do not jump into solution mode quickly. Instead, they ask themselves, "Which other factors are at play here?" They dig deeper and invite their team to develop solutions.

The ability to solving problems effectively boils down to the efficiency with which you apply your mind to the objective and to how much you use reason and logic. Persistence, focus, and imagination are key factors here. Keep an open mind. Seek comfort in the uncomfortable.

From:
Bicheno, J. (2009). *The Lean Games Book*. Buckinghamshire, England: Picsie Books.

Adapted by:
Dr. Silviana Falcon

HANDOUT #1

HANDOUT #2

HANDOUT #3

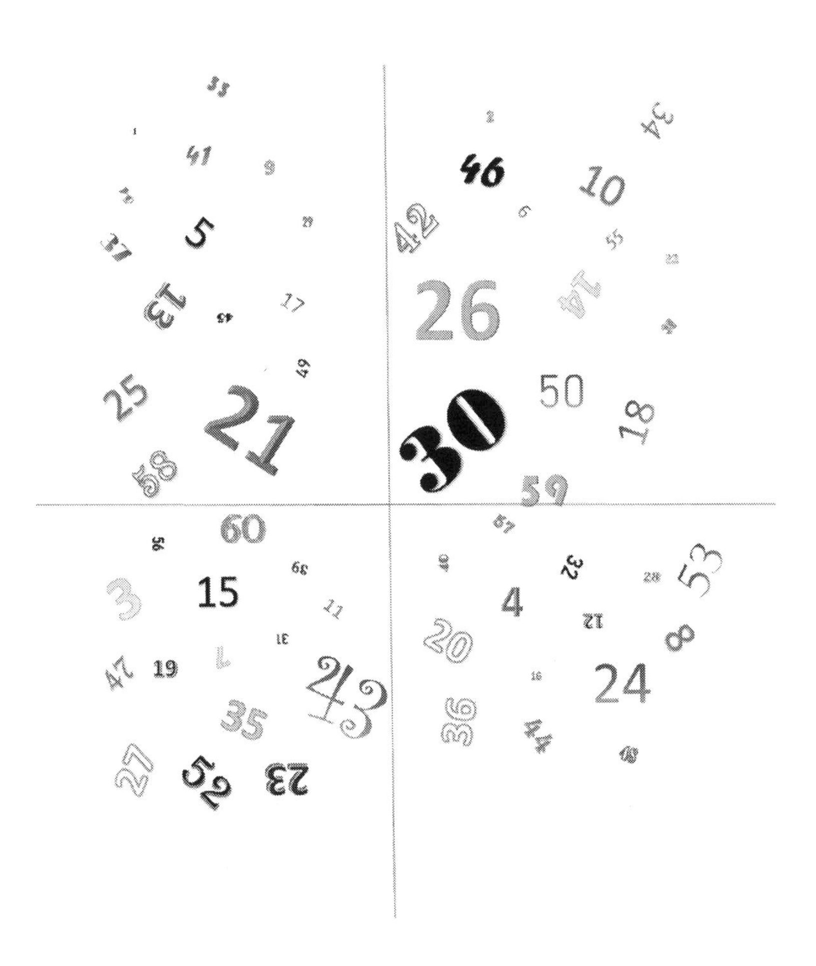

HANDOUT #4

1	2	3	4	5	6	7
8	9	10	11	12	13	14
15	16	17	18	19	20	21
22	23	24	25	26	27	28
29	30	31	32	33	34	35
36	37	38	39	40	41	42
43	44	45	46	47	48	49
50		52	53	54	55	56
57	58	59	60			

GAME: CULTURAL DIFFERENCES

INTRODUCTION:

This game is an adaptation of the classic cross-cultural game titled "Bafa Bafa" by D. Hicks.

PURPOSE/OBJECTIVE:

The game is intended to help students understand the implications cultural differences can have on commerce.

GROUP SIZE: Any.

MATERIALS:

Beta culture handout. Alpha culture handout. A red color sheet of paper. A blue color sheet of paper. A set of any books or product(s). Scotch Tape. Timer.

TIME: 50–60 minutes.

MUSIC: None.

PRE-GAME PROCEDURE:

1. Identify two rooms with easy access to each other (I have used one room for one group and the hallway for the second group). Identify one of the rooms as the Alpha Room and the second as the Beta Room.
2. Make copies of the Beta culture handout to give to each member of the Beta culture.

3. Make copies of the Alpha culture handout to give to each member of the Alpha culture.
4. In the Alpha culture room, tape the red color sheet of paper toward the back of the room, ensuring there is enough space for students to congregate. Tape the blue color sheet of paper toward the front of the room, ensuring there is enough space for students to congregate.
5. Use peel off clothing name tags to be worn by students to identify them as being a part of the Alpha or Beta culture.

PROCEDURE:

Share with all students that the objective of the activity is to successfully sell (have the other group buy) a product all while experiencing a cultural group different from their own.

Step 1: Divide students into two different groups: Alpha and Beta. Note: The two groups should be equal in number and gender mix; however, the Alpha culture cannot have more than 50 percent female students.

Step 2: Have the students separate into two groups in the respective room.

Step 3: The facilitator goes to the Alpha room and disseminates the Alpha culture handout along with the sticky labels for students to wear for easier identification as they play the game. Request the group studies and practices the traditions of their culture for fifteen to twenty minutes. They are also to elect three "observers" who will visit the Beta room later. Then, the facilitator goes to the Beta room and requests the group studies and practices the traditions of their culture for fifteen to twenty minutes. They are also to elect three "observers" who will visit the Alpha room later.

Step 4: Agree on a time (after the fifteen to twenty minutes) where the "observers" will visit each other's culture for five minutes. Let the "observers" know they are to find out as much about the culture they are visiting as possible, making sure they, themselves follow their own culture's practices and traditions.

Step 5: After five minutes, the facilitator goes into each of the two rooms and requests the "observers" return to their own home culture. They are to describe and interpret what they witnessed. This is the reflection period. As facilitator, move about both groups hearing the discussion and any points of confusion or discoveries they have made about the other culture. Allow five to six minutes for this reflection. At this time, students are really engaged trying to understand the other culture. Students are typically laughing and developing a strategy to determine more information with the next "observer" exchange.

Step 6. The facilitator starts another exchange of "observers" following step 5 above. More excitement ensues among students as the Alpha culture group develops a strategy to have the Beta culture group agree to buy their product.

Step 7. The facilitator starts the third and last exchange of "observers" following step 5 above. At this time, the discussion among students intensifies. Both groups are engaged. The Alpha culture is determined on developing a strategy to sell the product to the Beta culture.

Step 8. The facilitator brings the entire Beta culture group to the Alpha culture group room for the final interaction session. Allow for another five to ten minutes of interaction. Students are truly engaged at this point, trying to make a sale. In my experience facilitating this game, students use the written form (via a blackboard) to successfully communicate with one another and make the sale.

DISCUSSION QUESTIONS:

The discussion should be broadened to include all perceptions and assumptions made by each participant about the other culture. As facilitator, you can begin by asking:

- Beta culture students to explain their perceptions about the Alpha Culture.
- Alpha culture students to explain their perceptions about the Beta Culture.
- Alpha and Beta observers to share their thoughts and feelings when visiting the other culture group.
- What assumptions were made about the practices and behaviors of the other group? Were these assumptions helpful?
- Did the specific roles given to men and women in the Alpha culture cause any difficulties in cross culture relations?
- How important is language to effective communication between people?
- Has anyone been to another country where you have perceived the locals "behaving oddly?"

SUGGESTED LECTURE TOPICS:

- The social implications of diversity
- Diverse populations
- Ethnocentrism and other negative dynamics
- Doing business in a global arena

STUDENT LEARNING OBJECTIVES:

- Evaluate the challenges of cross-cultural communication.
- Create/develop awareness on cultural differences.

A LITTLE SAMPLE OF A LECTURE DISCUSSION:

This simple game reinforces the idea that cross-cultural communication is inherently difficult and conflictual. One of the most fruitful and interesting behaviors that evolved from this game is the way students attempted to manage interaction by compromising. For example, while both groups adhered fairly strictly to the speech cultural norms, the Alpha culture group tends to use gesturing in order to bridge the communication gap with the Beta culture group. But how much should each group compromise? What norms can be violated?

TAKEAWAYS:

Time and time again, the students react very positively to this simulation. They report having fun despite the obstacles of communication. More importantly, the post-exercise discussions and assessment tools indicate the exercise had value beyond what the students had learned in the lecture about cultural differences. Most students report a deeper learning of the difficulties inherent in cross-cultural communication, but also about their own assumptions and how they could be more sensitive to their own behavior in cross-cultural situations.

"A Cross Cultural Simulation Game" by Stephanie Thibeau and Bhreagh MacDonald.

https://e4sblog.files.wordpress.com/2018/10/bafa-bafa-a-cross-cultural-simulation-game.pdf

Adapted by:
Dr. Silviana Falcon

HANDOUTS:

ALPHA CULTURE

You will eventually meet all of the members of the Beta culture with the goal of successfully selling them a product (conduct trade). Your goal, as a good host, is to make all of the members of the Beta culture feel welcomed.

As a member of the Alpha culture, you have been raised with the following cultural norms:

1) Welcome new people with a handshake all while smiling and looking into the person's eyes. You should tell a joke to make them laugh. It is believed, the louder the laugh of the other person, the better the friendship will become.

2) It is only polite to speak and interact with the person of your own gender. One on one.

3) Two colors are important: blue and red. Blue is a place to meet for the first time. If you are interested in knowing or speaking with the person further, you should take them to the red area. You should never speak with someone who is in the red area first nor should you take them to the blue area.

4) Take the initiative to meet the new people. Make a point to shake each person's hand.

BETA CULTURE

You will eventually meet all of the members of the Alpha culture as they will be hosting you in their area. Your goal, as a good visitor, is to make all of the members of the Alpha culture feel appreciated.

As a member of the Beta culture, you have been raised with the following cultural norms:

1) It is improper to speak. All of your communication is generated via hand and body gestures.

2) If you want to speak with someone, you must point at them using your lips to signal your interest to engage in communication via gestures/body language.

3) It is improper to touch another person for any reason as germs can be passed on from one person to another. The best way to greet someone is by holding both of your hands and slightly bowing in front of each person you are greeting.

4) You have heard that the Alpha culture have a habit of touching other people and you grew up being told to distrust them.

5) Laughing in front of another person is insulting. You can only smile or gesture feeling pleased or happy.

GAME: INTERNATIONAL TRADING GAME

INTRODUCTION:

This game is a version of the World Trade Game, developed by the Third World development charity, Action. It is great for students in introductory courses in economics and international trade; however, it can be used and adapted for many other purposes.

PURPOSE/OBJECTIVE:

Countries compete against each other to "manufacture" paper shapes (circles, triangles, rectangles, etc.) and sell them to an international commodity market trader at posted prices, which vary with supply and demand. The objective for each country is to make as much money as possible.

GROUP SIZE: Between 20 and 60.

PRE-WORK:

Space: The game requires a large room, with loose tables and chairs.

The tables should be set so they are separated from one another. Here is a proposed diagram:

MATERIALS:

Monopoly money. 10x13 clasp manila envelopes. Rulers. Scissors. Compasses. Set square. Protractors. Pencils. 8½x11 copy paper. Commodities sheet handout. You will need to do five things:

1. Prepare an envelope of resources for each country:

You will need to fill each envelope with the appropriate materials in advance and label the envelope. All of the materials, including paper money, can be purchased at any office supply store. The following envelopes are required for each game.

Rich countries: A1, A2

2 pairs of scissors

2 rulers

1 compass

1 set square (the exact size of the large triangular shape)

1 protractor (the exact size of the semi-circular shape)

2 pencils

1 sheet of copy paper

6 × $100

Middle-income countries: B1, B2

2 pencils

1 ruler

10 sheets of copy paper

3 × $100

Low-income countries: C1, C2

2 pencils

4 sheets of copy paper

2 ×$100

2. Make copies of the commodity shapes, which show their measurements and their initial values and place one on each table (country). Handout below.
3. Prepare an envelope for the commodity trader which contains:

    1. The trader is given an envelope with money and a template of the shapes so that he/she can check whether the shapes are the right size. The template also gives the opening prices for the shapes.
    2. Money: 30 @ $50, 60 @ $100, 20 @ $500, 40 @ $1000.
    3. Pencil for marking changes to the prices of shapes.
    4. Large envelope for keeping completed shapes "secure."
    5. Notepad to document any loan advances.

4. Prepare a facilitator resource envelope containing:

    1. Whistle
    2. 8 small sticky notes
    3. 5 sheets printer paper per game

5. Prepare an easel board or use a white board and write the following information (Note: keep this information from the view of students until the end of the game):

- Divide the first page into four columns. On the first column, outline what was included in each team's (country's) envelope at the start of the game.
- On the second column, title the heading as, "What you have now." You will outline the resources each country owns at the end of the game and write them down by country.
- On the third column, write how much money they have at the end of the game.

TIME: 50–60 minutes.

MUSIC:

Upbeat music while students are working on creating their shapes.

PROCEDURE:

Step 1: Have students put away all of their belongings as they cannot use any of their personal items. All of what they will need to play the game will be provided to them.

Step 2: Ask for four volunteers. Two of whom will be the "observers" and two will work as the "traders."

Step 3: Once the four volunteers have been identified, the remaining students are divided into teams, each of which acts as a separate "country," with between two and ten students in each team. I have found that about six to seven students per group is the best number. There are five or six countries in a game.

Note:

For small groups: You can adjust the number of countries being represented; for example, have one rich country, two middle-income countries, and one low-income country.

For larger groups: You can play two games simultaneously with one facilitator so long as the rooms are close to one another.

Step 4: Have students go to their team table (country) and have the observers and traders come to the front of the room where you are.

Step 5. Give the following instructions about the game:

Each of the groups is a team, and each team represents a country. The objective for each country is to make as much money for itself as possible by using the materials in the envelope. As I distribute the materials, you can begin thinking about the name of your country. Please DO NOT open the folder until I start the game.

Once the materials have been distributed, obtain the students' attention once again and give the following instructions:

No other materials can be used. Use the materials to manufacture paper shapes. You can choose to make any of the shapes shown on the diagrams. A copy of the required diagrams is placed on each of your tables. All shapes must be cut with clean sharp edges using scissors and must be of the exact size specified on the diagrams. The shapes can be sold to the traders in batches, who will check them for accuracy and exchange them for cash. Inaccurate shapes will be rejected or will be paid for at a substantially lower rate.

You can manufacture as many shapes as you like—the more you make, the richer you will become. You must not cut up your envelope! You can move around the room but must not cross into the neighboring world(s), who are playing a parallel game.

If you hear me whistle [demonstrate], you must immediately stop what you are doing and pay attention. If there is any dispute, I will settle it. My word is final! No physical force is to be used in the game.

Give no further instructions. It is important for the students to work out what they should do.

Announce the start of manufacturing and tell them how long they have to play the game. Set your timer for fifteen minutes.

Step 4. While the students are beginning to play, meet with the two observers. Let them know that they are responsible for keeping order and letting you know if any unethical or unfair practices are being exhibited. They should note the formation and operation of any alliances and deals and any cheating that takes place. Observers should also report to you any situation. You, as the facilitator, decide if you can ignore or respond to the problem. Depending on the issue, you may choose to suspend a team from making shapes for five minutes or impose a monetary fine.

Have the observers keep notes of their observations so they can help debrief the session at the end. For example, get them to find out what is happening to the scissors, the paper, or any of the resources they have. What are each of the countries doing? How are the poor countries managing the lack of resources?

Step 5. While the observers begin their work, meet with the commodity traders. Share with the traders that they must be careful in measuring the shapes and reject any that have not been cut out. Alternatively, if they have been torn carefully against a ruler due to the lack of scissors, have them accept the commodity but pay a lesser price due to lack of quality. The traders decide on whether to accept the commodity and how much to pay for it. Note: I have had instances where a team steals money from the traders. Make sure the traders keep their envelope and purchased shapes away from the students' reach.

Let the traders know that you will announce when loans are available. If any country requests a loan, they are to keep record of them using the notepad provided. Loans will be available at a 50 percent interest rate. It is easiest for loans not to be repaid, but at the end of the game, when money is totaled, the trader will simply announce how much has to be deducted (outstanding loan plus interest) from each team.

AS A FACILITATOR:

Keep in regular contact with the traders. Find out which shapes are being produced more commonly (typically the triangles and rectangles) and which are not being produced (usually the circles and the protractor-sized semicircles). Then, blow the whistle and announce that, due to the forces of demand and supply, the prices of certain shapes have changed. Dramatically change the prices to encourage the production of shapes that are needed but not being produced (the prices are stipulated on the shape handout).

The discovery of raw materials in a developing country is simulated with the use of the sticky notes. **At fifteen minutes into the game**, give four small sticky shapes to each of the two low-income countries (or all eight to one of the low-income countries) and let them know that they can attach it to any of their shapes to triple the selling price (Note: as soon as the sticky notes are distributed, inform the traders and the observers of the new dimension added to the game). Set your timer for five minutes.

Once your five-minute timer goes off, announce that you will be holding an auction selling a pair of scissors. Although the poor countries would dearly like to buy a pair, one of the rich countries is more likely to be successful at the auction. As the game progresses, paper will rapidly run out. Therefore, announce a second auction selling five sheets of paper. At this point, students are all aware about the auction taking place and one person from the team usually stands up to participate in the auction while the rest of the team members continue developing shapes, the traders continue measuring and buying shapes, and the observers continue to take notes of the dynamics playing out.

ENDING THE GAME:

As the facilitator, provide a ten-minute warning of when the game will end. There will probably be a flurry of activity as students rush to make shapes with their remaining paper and bring those shapes to the commodity trader. After five minutes, provide a five-minute warning that the game will end. Anyone with shapes and already lined up at the trader's table will be able to sell their shapes. No other completed shapes after the end of the game can be sold. While the last of the shapes are being sold, ask the observers to begin adding the money each country has and write it down.

DEBRIEF/DISCUSSION QUESTIONS:

Allocate about ten to fifteen minutes to debrief the game. Any more time will drain the energy created by the game. However, the debriefing session needs to be planned as carefully as the activity.

DEBRIEFING PROCESS:

Use the whiteboard to guide the initial conversation. Share with all students the resources each of the countries had at the onset of the game (which had been previously recorded by you). Next, have each team share what resources they had left at the end of the game. And third, have each team report how much money they had at the end of the game. This information must be certified verbally by the observers.

Here are some suggested questions:

- What are some of the similarities and the differences from the beginning to the end in terms of resources?
- What are some of the insights from the observers? What were the best strategies used by the various countries? What worked best?
- How does this game simulate the real world?
- Do you think there is a need for treaties and alliances?
- As the facilitator, you can develop more questions based on the desired learning outcomes for the activity.

Suggested Lecture Topics:

- The importance of market power in international trade
- The importance of trade alliances

- Global trade mechanisms
- Price determinations related to supply and demand
- Derived demand and price of inputs
- Game theory

Student Learning Objectives:

- Evaluate collaboration and working in teams.
- Appraise and analyze opportunity cost.
- Appraise and analyze price elasticity.
- Analyze and react to supply and demand forces.
- Appraise the law of comparative advantage.
- Appraise world inequality.
- Appraise trade issues within developing countries.
- Analyze the concept of powerlessness (hopelessness).
- Analyze the concept of greed.
- Analyze economic behavior.
- Analyze trade agreements.

Source:
John Sloman
University of the West of England
john.sloman@bristol.ac.uk
Published September 2002
https://www.economicsnetwork.ac.uk/showcase/sloman_game

Adapted by:
Dr. Silviana Falcon

COMMODITIES HANDOUT

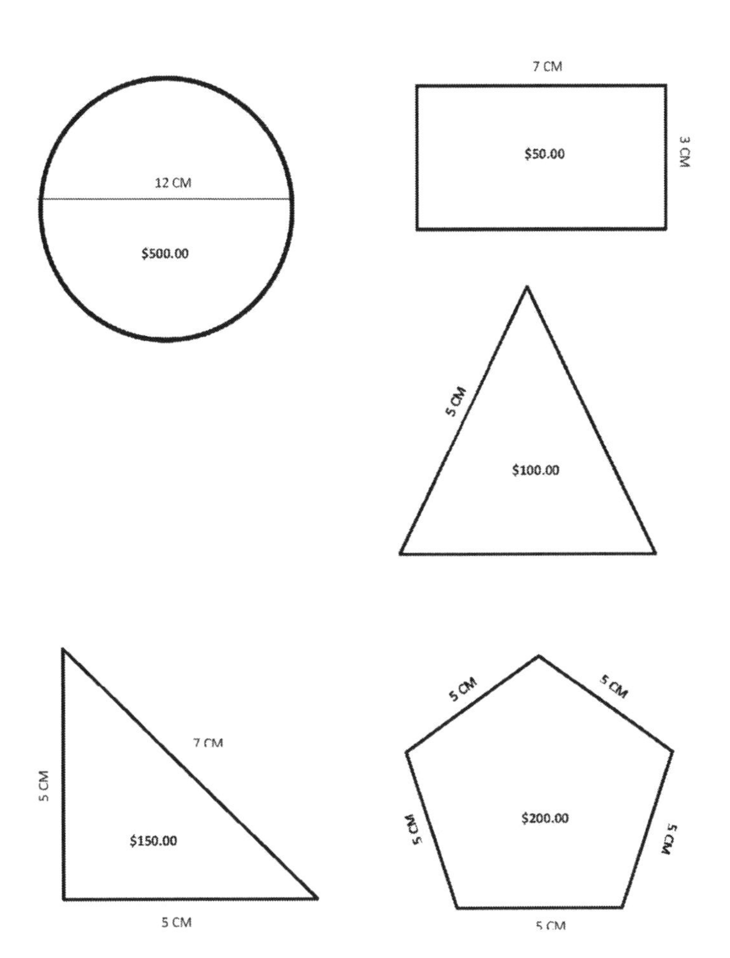

GAME: STARPOWER

INTRODUCTION:

This is a complex game to set up and carry out, but it is well worth the effort. It entails students engaging in chip trading in order to accumulate more wealth and thus, achieve more influence and power. This exercise simulates systems of power, privilege, and oppression. The game raises students' awareness and knowledge about power differentials within society.

PURPOSE/OBJECTIVE:

First developed in the 1960s (Shirts 1969), StarPower creates a limited-mobility, three-tiered society based on differential wealth. Students engage in "chip trading sessions" to increase their individual wealth and societal status. Students have an opportunity to exchange chips with other students in order to enhance their scores. Although most students remain in their original group throughout the game, there is a bonus option that sometimes allows a lower status person an upward mobility opportunity. After several trading rounds, the wealthy group "earns" the right to make rules for the rest of the game and trading continues under the new established rules.

GROUP SIZE:

Any, but preferably between 20 and 35.

MATERIALS:

The StarPower Game kit comes with all of the instructions and tokens needed. You can find it from various providers by searching StarPower game simulation.

TIME: 60 minutes.

PROCEDURE:

Players randomly draw lots of colored chips. These chips have different number value based on their color. Players are given the opportunity to trade these chips over "trading rounds" to increase their point total. Players are told not share information about their chips. Players are told their classification or group assignment is based on "achievement" or "merit," but in reality, the initial distribution of chips is intended to skew the resulting scores.

Each round, players draw random colored chips and trade them for sets of points. At the end of each round, players are assigned one of three groups based on the number of points they have. The top scorers are red squares, the middle are blue circles, and the low scorers are green triangles.

Starting on turn two (the first turn in which players are assigned to groups), the facilitator ensures that the red squares players draw from a bag with higher scoring chips, while the green triangles draw from a bag with lower scoring chips, without letting the students know this is the case. As a result, movement between groups becomes uncommon. Starting on the third round, the red squares are free to change the rules however they like.

One of the most important aspects linked to the educational effectiveness of this game is making sure that the facilitator does not tell the players early on that the red squares will be able to change the rules. This is extremely important because some of the concepts the game helps to illustrate the complexities associated with economic, social, and political stratification, linkages between wealth and power, how stratification is maintained and justified, and how it is experienced on personal and as collective members of a different level or social strata.

DISCUSSION NOTES/QUESTIONS:

I have played this game several times with much success. One adaptation I have made to this game is that I place a significant number of extra points to be awarded to the winners. This adds a lot of competition among students.

Students' emotional responses are varied. The "triangles" (lower class) tend to become very resentful, especially when the rules are changed by the "squares" (wealthy class). In my experience, students just either give up or inquire as to how to "move" away or migrate out of the system, which is interesting as a way to have students "feel" the struggles of a decision made by immigrants across the globe. In recent years, I have had students in the square strata change the outcome by deciding to redistribute "wealth," and in essence, create an egalitarian society.

This game also is great at illustrating complex processes of economic, social, and political stratification as well as linkages between wealth and political power. StarPower can also illustrate how race, ethnicity, gender, or other visible social identity markers function in stratified societies.

It is very important to stop the game with enough time to have a ten- to fifteen-minute discussion, allowing the students to process how they are feeling before beginning to link the activity to an academic topic or lecture. Often, I just let students talk aloud and build on one another's points. I ask students to complete the one-minute paper exercise because it allows students who are more reserved to reflect and "voice" their reactions. A one-minute paper is a very short paper students write in a minute in response to one or more prompts from the instructor. For this exercise, I use it more as a free form, letting students simply react to the day's lesson and write whatever comes to mind for that minute. I typically use the learnings from this experience during a variety of lectures throughout the course of the semester.

SUGGESTED LECTURE TOPICS:

- Leadership and power
- Immigration
- Political rules and implications on society
- Learned helplessness
- Ethics
- Diversity and Inclusion

Source:
Simulations for Schools and Charities. StarPower: Use & Abuse of Power, Leadership & Diversity. Retrieved February 14, 2021.
https://www.simulationtrainingsystems.com/schools-and-charities/products/starpower/

ACKNOWLEDGMENTS

Lectures and Play, like all books, was a team effort. I am grateful to Eric Koester, professor of practice at Georgetown University's McDonough School of Business, for his extraordinary vision and courage to create a successful platform for all aspiring authors. His team at New Degree Press was a delight to work with: my brilliant editors, Amanda Munro and Paige Bauxbaum, as well as the entire publishing and creative team. You all rock!

Special thanks to friends who took the time to read the manuscript and offer their advice: Dr. Susan Freeman, Dr. Michael Weber, Cynthia Sternlicht, and Nyrka Riskin, as well as the many friends from whom I have learned to be human and a better teacher: Dr. Kira Omelchenko, Dr. Sue McNamara, Dr. Sara Terrell, Dr. Melissa Garr, Dr. Michael Kennedy, Dr. Bruce Darby, Dr. Kyle Fedler, Dr. Autumn Grubb, Dr. Rebecca Powell, Dr. Lori Rakes, Dr. Susan Banks, Dr. Lisa Ghaly, Dr. Kandi Wiens, Dr. Cindy Hardin, and Professor Celina Jozsi.

I would also like to thank those who supported my dream by pre-ordering my book: Terry Rose, Brenda C. Bailey, Kathryn

Dumont, Patricia Sheck, Julie Goodwin, Erick Hernandez, Maria Elena Zas, Carlos Borde, Julia M. Borum, Gerlinde Dancy, Joy Williams, Madison Campbell, Judy Gentry, AndrewPaul McIntosh, Jazmine Everheart, Ilona Kauffman, Wanda McManus, Cynthia Sternlicht, and Shari Brown.

A final and most heartfelt thanks to my husband, Raul Falcon, my sons, Jessie, Riley, Reece, and my mother, Sylviana Hernandez for always being the wind beneath my wings.

APPENDIX

Busteed, Brandon. "Higher Education's Work Preparation Paradox." *Gallup*. February 25, 2014. https://news.gallup.com/opinion/gallup/173249/higher-education-work-preparation-paradox.aspx.

Deslauriers, Louis, McCarty, Logan, Miller, Kelly, Callaghan, Kristina, and Kestin, Greg. "Measuring Actual Learning versus Feeling of Learning in Response to Being Actively Engaged in the Classroom." *Proceedings of the National Academy of Sciences USA*. 116, no. 39 (September 2019): 19251–19257.

Deslauriers, Louis, Schelew, Elen, and Wieman, Carl. "Improved Learning in a Large-Enrollment Physics Class." *Science* 332, no. 6031 (May 2011): 862–864.

Forbes, Lisa K. "The Process of Play in Learning in Higher Education: A Phenomenological Study," *Journal of Teaching and Learning* 15. no. 1 (2021): 57-73.

Freeman, Scott, Eddy, Sarah L., McDonough, Miles, Smith, Michelle K., Okoroafor, Nnadozie, Jordt, Hannah, and

Wenderoth, Mary Pat. “Active Learning Increases Student Performance in Science, Engineering, and Mathematics.” *Proceedings of the National Academy of Sciences USA* 111. no. 23 (June 2014): 8410–8415.

Hake, Richard. “Interactive-Engagement versus Traditional Methods: A Six-Thousand-Student Survey of Mechanics Test Data for Introductory Physics Courses.” *American Journal of Physics* 66, no. 2 (January 1998): 64–74.

Handelsman, Jo, Miller Sarah, and Pfund, Christine. *A Manual for the Scientific (Teaching) Revolution. (New York: W. H. Freeman and Company, 2007), 184.*

Knight, Jennifer K. and William B. Wood. “Teaching More by Lecturing Less.” *Cell Biology Education* 4, *no. 4 (*Winter 2005): 298–310.

National Research Council. *How People Learn: Brain, Mind, Experience and School.* Washington, DC: *National Academies Press;* (2000).

Petersen, Christina I., Beits, Al, Ching, Paul, Gorman, Kristen S., Neudauer, Cheryl L., Rozaitis, William, Walker, J.D. and Wingert, Deb. “The Tyranny of Content: “Content Coverage” as a Barrier to Evidence-Based Teaching Approaches and Ways to Overcome It.“ *Life Sciences Education* 19. no. 2 (May 15, 2020).

Prince, Michael. “Does Active Learning Work? A Review of the Research.”*Journal of Engineering Education* 93, no. 3 (July 2004): 223–231.

US Chamber of Commerce. *Learning to Work. Working to Learn.* Washington, DC: US Chamber of Commerce. Foundation. https://www.uschamberfoundation.org/sites/default/files/Learning%20to%20Work%20Working%20to%20Learn.pdf.

CHAPTER 1.

Arum, Richard and Roksa, Juptin. *Academically Adrift: Limited Learning on College Campuses.* (New York and London: University Chicago Press, 2011).

Bransford, John D., Brown,Ann L., and Cocking, Rodney R. "*How People Learn: Brain, Mind, Experience, and School: Expanded Edition. National Research Council. (Washington, D.C.,* National Academy Press, 2000).

Brown, Stuart. "*Play: How it Shapes the Brain, Opens the Imagination, and Invigorates the Soul*". (New York: The Penguin Group, 1979).

Brown, Stuart. "Play is More than Just Fun, Stuart Brown, Ted Talk." Ted Talks, 8 May 2008, https://www.ted.com/talks/stuart_brown_play_is_more_than_just_fun?language=en.

Eyler, Joshua R. *How Humans Learn: The Science and Stories behind Effective College Teaching* (West Virginia University Press, 2018): 86.

Forbes, Lisa. "The Process of Play In Learning in Higher Education: A Phenomenological Study," *Journal of Teaching and Learning* 15, no.1 (2021):57-73.

Finkel, Donald L. *Teaching with Your Mouth Shut.* (Portsmouth, NH: Boyton/Cook Publishers, 2000).

Konopka, Clovis Luis, Adaime, Martha Bohrer, and Mosele, Pedro Henrique, "Active Teaching and Learning Methodologies: Some Considerations" *Creative Education* 06, no. 14 (January 2015):1536-1545.

Lappe Frances Moore and Perkins, Jeffrey. *You Have the Power: Choosing Courage in a Culture of Fear* (New York: Jeremy P. Tarcher/Penguin Group USA, 2005). 151-176.

Major, Claire H., Harris, Michael S., and Zakrajsek, Todd. *Teaching for Learning (New York: Routledge, 2015).*

Orbach, Eliezer, "Simulation Games and Motivation for Learning: A Theoretical Framework," *Simulation & Games* 10, no. 1 (March 1979): 3–40. https://doi.org/10.1177/003755007910100l.

Pascarella, Ernest and Blaich, Charles. "Lessons from the Wabash National Study of Liberal Arts Education, Change." *The Magazine of Higher Learning* 45, no. 2, (March 2013).

Petranek, Clovis Luis, Corey, Susan, and Black, Rebecca. "Three Levels of Learning in Simulations: Participating, Debriefing, and Journal Writing," *Simulation & Gaming* 23, no. 2: 174-185. <http://hdl.handle.net/2027.42/69040.

The 2019 Student Survey Report (Executive Summary). Prepared by National Association of Colleges and Employers (Bethlehem, PA, 2019). https://www.naceweb.org/

uploadedfiles/files/2019/publication/executive-summary/2019-nace-student-survey-four-year-executive-summary.pdf.

Vandercruysse, Slyke, Vandewaetere, Mieke, and Clarebout, Geraldine, "Game-Based Learning: A Review on the Effectiveness of Educational Games," In M.M. Cruz-Cunha (Eds.), *Handbook of Research on Serious Games as Educational, Business, and Research Tools: 628-647.* https://www.academia.edu/23148569/Game-Based_Learning.

CHAPTER 2.

Bransford, John D., Brown,Ann L., and Cocking, Rodney R. "*How People Learn: Brain, Mind, Experience, and School: Expanded Edition. National Research Council. (Washington, D.C.,* National Academy Press, 2000).

Cengage. "New Survey: Demand for "Uniquely Human Skills" Increases Even as Technology and Automation Replace Some Jobs." Cengage press release, January 16, 2019. Cengage website. https://news.cengage.com/upskilling/new-survey-demand-for-uniquely-human-skills-increases-even-as-technology-and-automation-replace-some-jobs/.

Handelsman, Jo, Miller Sarah, and Pfund, Christine. *A Manual for the Scientific (Teaching) Revolution," (New York: W. H. Freeman and Company, 2007), 184.*

National Association of Colleges and Employers. "The Top Attributes Employers Want to See on Resumes." National Association of Colleges and Employers press release, January 13, 2021. National Association of Colleges and Employers website. https://www.naceweb.org/talent-acquisition/candidate-selection/key-attributes-employers-want-to-see-on-students-resumes/.

Postal, Leslie. "'Test Banks' are at the Center of UCF's Cheating Scandal," *Orlando Sentinel*, November 21, 2010. https://www.orlandosentinel.com/news/os-xpm-2010-11-21-os-ucf-cheating-online-20101121-story.html.

Willis, Judy. "*Brain-Based Teaching Strategies for Improving Students' Memory, Learning, and Test-Taking Success.*" Childhood Education 83, no. 5 (2007): 310-315, DOI: 10.1080/00094056.2007.10522940.

The World University Rankings. "Global Employability University Rankings and Survey 2020 Released." Times Higher Education press release, November 19, 2020. Times Higher Education website.https://www.timeshighereducation.com/academic/press-releases/global-employability-university-ranking-and-survey-2020-released-1.

CHAPTER 3:

Acunso, Jay. "Never Feed Salad to a Lion: What Great Creators Know that Others Forget." *Marketing Showrunners,* April 18, 2018.

Bain, Ken. *What the Best College Teachers Do. Harvard University Press.* 2004.

Claxton, Guy, and Bill Lucas. *Educating Ruby: What Our Children Really Need to Learn.* Crown House Publishing. 2015.

Confrey, Jere. "A review of the Research on Student Conceptions in Mathematics, Science, and Programming" *Review of Research and Education* 16, no. 2 (1990): 3-56.

Freeman, S., Eddy, S.L., McDonough, M., Smith, M.K., Okoroafor, N., Jordt, H., Wenderoth, M.P. *Active learning boosts performance in STEM courses.* Proceedings of the National Academy of Sciences Jun 2014, 111 (23) 8410-8415; DOI: 10.1073/pnas.1319030111.

Grant, Adam. *Think Again: The Power of Knowing What You Don't Know.* Viking, 2021.

Honeycutt, Barbi; "5 Ways to Break Your Lecture with the 321 Strategy"; *Lecture Breakers* (blog); 2021. https://barbihoneycutt.com/blogs/lecture-breakers-blog/5-ways-to-break-your-lecture-with-the-321-strategy.

Honeycutt, Barbi. "Episode 80: Student Engagement Techniques (Part 2) with Dr. Claire Howell Major." Lecture Breakers; 2021. https://barbihoneycutt.com/blogs/podcast/episode-80-student-engagement-techniques-part-2-with-dr-claire-howell-major.

Jacobs, Jerry (2004). The Faculty Time Divide. *Sociological Forum, 19*(1), 3-27. Retrieved June 22, 2021. http://www.jstor.org/stable/4148805.

Jones, Justice. "Students to Mix Potions with Reality in New Harry Potter-Themed Chemistry Class." *The Daily Nebraskan,* November 20, 2011. http://www.dailynebraskan.com/news/students-to-mix-potions-with-reality-in-new-harry-potter-themed-chemistry-class/article_d768c987-c1f1-50de-9904-8a97df8fa477.html.

Lionni, Leo. *Fish is Fish.* (New York: Alfred Knopf, 1970).

Lucas, Bill. *Rethinking Assessment in Education: The Case for Change.* Center for Strategic Education, 2021.

https://drive.google.com/file/d/16qKudSF7qKRpgLOc5Ut3XeNjPl7Ni39n/view.

Minstrell, James A. "Teaching Science for Understanding." *REPORT NO PUB DATE NOTE AVAILABLE FROM* (1989): 129.

Simon Sinek, comment on How to Simplify Concepts So You Can Teach Them. January 9, 2014. https://www.youtube.com/watch?v=e4PGwQU-1Yc.

Stanger-Hall, Kathrin F. "Multiple-choice exams: an obstacle for higher-level thinking in introductory science classes." *CBE—Life Sciences Education* 11, no. 3 (2012): 294-306.

CHAPTER 4:

Carnegie, Andrew. "The Gospel of Wealth, 1889." *Profiles in Audacity: Great Decisions and how They Were Made* (2006): 269.

Gaiman, Neil. "The Art of Story Telling." Episode 1. Master Class, 2021. https://www.masterclass.com/classes/neil-gaiman-teaches-the-art-of-storytelling.

Haven, Kendall. *Story Proof: The Science behind the Startling Power of Story.* Greenwood Publishing Group, 2007.

Lapierre, Dominique. *The city of joy.* Random House, 1992.

Oats, Joyce Carol. "The Art of Short Story." Episode 5. Master Class, 2021. https://www.masterclass.com/classes/joyce-carol-oates-teaches-the-art-of-the-short-story.

Stephens, Greg J., Lauren J. Silbert, and Uri Hasson. "Speaker–listener neural coupling underlies successful communication." *Proceedings of the National Academy of Sciences* 107, no. 32 (2010): 14425-14430.

CHAPTER 5:

Brown, Brené. *The Power of Vulnerability: Teachings on Authenticity, Connection and Courage.* Audio Book by Sounds True, 2012.

Korn, Melissa. "How to Teach Professors Humility? Hand Them a Rubik's Cube". *Wall Street Journal,* February 26, 2021.

Lam, Sherrell T., and Cristin A. Mount. "Leading Through Times of Famine." *Military medicine* (2019).

Rodriguez, Vanessa. "The potential of systems thinking in teacher reform as theorized for the teaching brain framework." *Mind, Brain, and Education* 7, no. 2 (2013): 77-85.

You Tube. "Brené Brown on Empathy and Sympathy," April 1, 2016. https://www.youtube.com/watch?v=KZBTYViDPlQ.

CHAPTER 6:

"Amazon Alexa: Pompeii". You Tube video, April 20, 2021. https://www.youtube.com/watch?v=Kwhr1U-Ncv4.

Bersin, Josh. "Why Skills-Based Learning is not Enough: Building Capabilities for the Future of Work." Novoed. January 16, 2020. https://www.novoed.com/resources/webinars/why-skills-based-learning-is-not-enough-building-capabilities-for-the-future-of-work/.

Boyer, Ernest, L. "Creating the New American College," *Chronicle of Higher Education*, March 9, 1994. https://www.chronicle.com/article/creating-the-new-american-college/.

"Building Tomorrow's Talent: Collaboration Can Close the Emerging Skills Gap." Bureau of National Affairs (2018). http://unitedwayswva.org/wp-content/uploads/2019/07/Building-Tomorrows-Talent-Collaboration-Can-Close-Emerging-Skills-Gap.pdf.

Burning Glass Technologies and Strada Institute for the Future of Work. "The Permanent Detour: Underemployment's Long-Term Effects on the Careers of College Grads." (2018).

Byrne, John. Gies' iMBA: Inside A Disruptive Online MBA Option. Poets & Quants, August 12, 2020. https://www.nvcc.edu/news/press-releases/2018/amazon-apprenticeship-cohort.html.

Camorro-Premuzic, Thomas and Becky Frankiewicz. "Does Higher Education Still Prepare People for Jobs?." *Harvard Business Review,* January 7, 2019, updated January 14, 2019. https://hbr.org/2019/01/does-higher-education-still-prepare-people-for-jobs.

"College Enrollment and Retention in the Era of COVID." *The College Board* (2020). https://research.collegeboard.org/pdf/enrollment-retention-covid2020.pdf.

Courant, P.N., Turner, S. (2017). *Faculty Deployment in Research Universities.* National Bureau of Economic Research.

Enactus. "Our Story." accessed January 5, 2021. https://enactus.org/who-we-are/our-story/.

Gronseth, Susie, Waneta Herbert. "GroupMe; Investigating Use of Mobile Instant Messaging in Higher Education Courses." *Tech Trends* 63, (December 2018). https://www.researchgate.net/publication/329757412_GroupMe_Investigating_Use_of_Mobile_Instant_Messaging_in_Higher_Education_Courses.

Grow with Google. "Google IT Certificates." Accessed December 10, 2020. https://grow.google/programs/it-support/#/!?modal_active=none.

Gyurko, Jonathan, Penny MacCormack, Martha M. Bless, Jaqueline Jodl. *Why Colleges and Universities Need to Invest in Quality Teaching More than Ever.* American Council of Education, 2016. http://acue.org/wp-content/uploads/2018/07/ACUE-White-Paper1.pdf.

Korn, Melissa and Douglas Belkin. "College Admission Season is Crazier Than Ever. That Could Change Who Gets In." *Wall Street Journal,* March 16, 2021.https://www.wsj.com/articles/college-admission-season-is-crazier-than-ever-that-could-change-who-gets-in-11615909061.

"Learn More, Earn more: Education leads to higher wages, lower unemployment," *Career Outlook,* U.S. Bureau of Labor Statistics, May 2020. https://www.bls.gov/careeroutlook/2020/data-on-display/education-pays.htm.

Ma, Jennifer, Matea Pender, and Meredith Welch. "Trends in Higher Education: Education Pays 2019." *College Board* (2019). https://research.collegeboard.org/pdf/education-pays-2019-full-report.pdf.

McKenzie, Lindsay. "At Home, Workers See Alternative Credentials.'" *Inside Higher Education,* August 10, 2020. https://www.insidehighered.com/news/2020/08/10/surge-alternative-credentials-holds-steady-now.

ManpowerGroup, 2016-2017 Talent Shortage Survey, 2017

Miller, A. (2016). Building upon the components of academic advising to facilitate change. In T. Grites, M. Miller, J. Voller (Eds.), *Beyond foundations: Developing as a master academic advisor* (50-51). Hoboken, NJ: John Wiley & Sons.

National Student Clearinghouse. "Spring 2021 Enrollment (As of March 25)." Internet & Research. Updated April 29, 2021. https://nscresearchcenter.org/stay-informed/.

Nova, Annie. "Why your First Job out of College Really, Really Matters." *CNBC,* January 26, 2018, updated July 2, 2018. https://www.cnbc.com/2018/06/25/why-your-first-job-out-of-college-really-really-matters.html.

"NOVA Collaborates with Amazon Web Services to Create Associates Degree with Cloud Computing Specialization."

June 20, 2018. https://www.nvcc.edu/news/press-releases/2018/aws-cloud.html.

Reich, J., Ruperes-Valiente, J. (2019) *"The MOOC Pivot"* *Science* 363, no. 6423 (2019): 130-131. https://science.sciencemag.org/content/363/6423/130?utm_source=e-Literate+Newsletter&utm_campaign=fd7c2d2185-RSS_EMAIL_CAMPAIGN&utm_medium=email&utm_term=0_deab6fbf84-fd7c2d2185-40282373.

Romano, Benjamin. "Amazon Teams with City University of Seattle to Train Military Employees for New Roles." *The Seattle Times,* August 26, 2020.https://www.seattletimes.com/business/amazon/amazon-teams-with-city-university-of-seattle-to-train-military-employees-for-new-roles/.

Sedmak, Todd. "Fall 2020 Undergraduate Enrollment Down 4% Compared to Same Time Last Year." *National Student Clearing House,* October 15, 2020.https://www.studentclearinghouse.org/blog/fall-2020-undergraduate-enrollment-down-4-compared-to-same-time-last-year/.

St. Armour, Madeline. "Report: Enrollment Continue to Trend Downward." *Inside Higher Education*, October 15, 2020. https://www.insidehighered.com/news/2020/10/15/worrying-enrollment-trends-continue-clearinghouse-report-shows.

Ziker, John P., Allyanna Wintermote, David Nolin, Kathryn Demps, Matthew Genuchi, and Katie Meinhardt. "Time distribution of faculty workload at Boise State University." (2014).

Zimmerman, Eli. "College Pivot to Train Tomorrow's IT Experts." *ED Tech*, July 5, 2018. https://edtechmagazine.com/

higher/article/2018/07/colleges-pivot-train-tomorrows-it-experts.

Zinsheteyn, Mikhail. "Community Colleges Work with Google to Offer Tech Training." *US News & World Report,* March 09, 2020. https://www.usnews.com/news/best-states/articles/2020-03-09/community-colleges-offer-google-it-certificate.

CHAPTER 7:

Bachman, Leonard, and Christine Bachman. "A study of classroom response system clickers: Increasing student engagement and performance in a large undergraduate lecture class on architectural research." *Journal of Interactive Learning Research* 22, no. 1 (2011): 5-21.

Bonwell, Charles C., and James A. Eison. "Active Learning: Creating Excitement in the Classroom. ERIC Digest." (1991).

Casarosa, Enrico. (Director). (2020). *Luca.*

Deresiewicz, William (2016) *Excellent Sheep.* New York: Free Press.

Fisher, Douglas, Nancy Frey, Russell J. Quaglia, Dominique Smith, and Lisa L. Lande. *Engagement by design: Creating learning environments where students thrive.* Corwin Press, 2017.

Kolb, D. A. *(1984). Experiential Learning: Experience as the Source of Learning and Development.* New Jersey: Prentice Hall.

Machemer, Patricia L., and Pat Crawford. "Student perceptions of active learning in a large cross-disciplinary classroom." *Active learning in higher education* 8, no. 1 (2007): 9-30.

Parker, Priya (2020). *The Art of Gathering: How We Meet and Why It Matters.* New York: Riverhead Books.

Prince, Michael. "Does active learning work? A review of the research." *Journal of engineering education* 93, no. 3 (2004): 223-231.

Roberto, Michael. " Getting – and Then Keeping – Students Engaged". Webinar from Harvard Business Publishing Education, online, March 31, 2021.

Schoel, J., Prouty, D., & Radcliffe, P. (1988). *Islands of Healing: A Guide to Adventure Based Counseling.* Hamilton, MA: Project Adventure.

Streisand, B. (Director). (1996). *The Mirror Has Two Faces.*

Made in the USA
Columbia, SC
01 August 2023